THEN AND THERE
GENERAL EDITOR
MARJORIE REEVES

D1766657

Russia under the Last Tsar

HEATHER CUBITT

Illustrated from contemporary sources

LONGMAN

LONGMAN GROUP LIMITED
Longman House,
Burnt Mill, Harlow, Essex CM20 2JE, England
and Associated Companies throughout the World.

First published 1980
Third impression 1984
ISBN 0 582 22141 2

Set in 11/12½ Baskerville, Monophoto 169

Printed in Hong Kong by
Astros Printing Ltd

For Vera Petrovna

ound Filmstrip: History of Russia

ite filmstrips giving a short visual
odern Russia. Part 3 is the most

g, 1700–1856
857–1917
964

Contents

To the Reader

'Russia is a *cauldron* of boiling water, tightly closed and placed on a fire which is becoming hotter and hotter. I fear an explosion.'

This is what a French traveller to St Petersburg, Russia's former capital, (now called Leningrad) wrote in 1830. The cauldron of unrest continued to simmer for the rest of the century. Finally the explosion came. The Emperor of Russia, the Tsar, was overthrown in a *revolution* in 1917.

Revolutions occur when the ruler completely fails to understand the needs and hopes of his people. He does not carry out the changes and reforms needed to satisfy them. What had gone wrong in Russia under Nicholas II? Could such violence have been prevented?

In this book you will discover why there was a revolution in 1917. How the revolutionaries carried it out, and what happened afterwards, is described more fully in another book in this series 'Lenin and the Russian Revolution'.

Words printed in *italics* are explained in the Glossary on page 92.

Opposite: *The Russian Empire under Tsar Nicholas II*

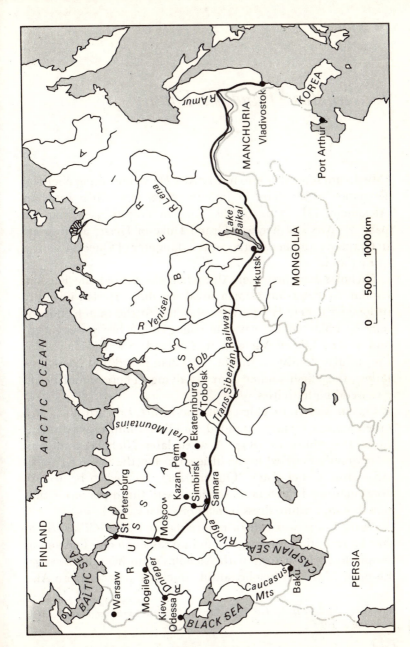

1 *Nicholas II and his Family*

'My dream some day is to marry Alix H', wrote young Nicholas Romanov in his diary in January 1892. His father was Tsar Alexander III, ruler of the Russian empire (see map on page 5). Alix's father was Grand Duke of Hesse, a tiny state in Germany and her mother was a daughter of Queen Victoria of England.

Nicholas had first met Alix when she visited the Russian capital, St Petersburg, for a royal wedding. He fell instantly in love with her. His parents objected to the match, but for once Nicholas had his way. The young couple became engaged, and visited Queen Victoria in England. Shortly afterwards they returned sadly to Russia. They had heard that Nicholas's father, the harsh soldier Tsar lay dying. There would be no gay wedding festivities.

Queen Victoria's eldest son, the future Edward VII, and other foreign royalty attended the Tsar's impressive funeral in St Petersburg in 1894. A week later Nicholas and Alix were quietly married in the little chapel at the Winter Palace. Alix wrote to her sister, 'Our marriage seemed to be a mere continuation of the funeral service – with this difference – that now I wore a white dress instead of a black one.'

As the court was still in mourning for the late Tsar, there was no reception afterwards, and no honeymoon. The young couple lived for a time with Nicholas's mother, the *Dowager* Empress Maria in her beautiful Anichkov palace. Here Alix

Opposite: *Nicholas II, the last Tsar of Russia, who was overthrown in the revolution of 1917*

was dominated by her mother-in-law, and Nicholas by his awe-inspiring, over-powering uncles.

The coronation the following May was spoiled by tragedy. After the solemn ceremony in Moscow cathedral (where Tsars were always crowned) celebrations continued for three days. Royalty, ambassadors and 7,000 important people enjoyed themselves at splendid balls and banquets. Meanwhile thousands of working people gathered on the great plain outside the city. Nicholas had promised to give everyone little presents. Rumours spread that the gifts were running short, and crowds of people surged forward. Hundreds were crushed to death, and the meadow was littered with corpses. Nicholas and Alix were terribly upset, but were persuaded by members of the royal family to attend a ball given that evening by the French ambassador: they must not offend France. They visited the injured in hospital the next day, but many people considered them cold and heartless, and never forgave them. Nicholas and Alix were always to be out of touch, cut off from their people.

Alix, now called Alexandra, was tall, slim and beautiful, with red-gold hair and sensitive grey eyes. She held herself with great dignity and poise, but she was shy in company, and people thought her cold and proud. She hated court ceremony, and large gatherings and formal parties gave her nervous sick headaches. The French ambassador remembered the Tsarina once at an official banquet, beautiful in a low *brocade* gown, a diamond *tiara* on her head, but he noticed that 'her smile became set, and the veins stood out on her cheeks. She bit her lips every minute through nervousness.'

Alexandra was very religious. After her marriage she gave up her Protestant faith, and became a devout member of the Russian *Orthodox Church*. She loved her new country, and learnt the Russian language, though she spoke English at home, as she had been brought up in a thoroughly English way by her English mother.

The Tsar and Tsarina had four daughters: Olga was clever, strong-willed, rather hot-tempered; Maria plump and sweet-natured; Tatiana tall, slender, beautiful like her mother. Anastasia, the youngest, was full of fun, a real tomboy. But Nicholas and Alexandra longed for a son.

When in 1904 the long-awaited boy, Alexei, was born, tragedy struck the family. Alexei had haemophilia, an extremely rare blood disease which prevents blood from clotting: the slightest bump can cause bleeding which is very hard to stop. The disease can be passed to male members of a family through their mothers. Several members of Queen Victoria's family inherited it, and Alexandra could never forgive herself that she was responsible for the ill-health of her beloved Alexei. This worry added to her shyness and unhappiness.

The baby was only six weeks old when the first signs of haemophilia were discovered. Nicholas wrote in his diary, 'Alix and I have been very worried. Bleeding began this morning without the slightest cause from the navel of our small Alexei. It lasted with but a few interruptions until evening.'

The Tsarevich, as the Tsar's eldest son is called, often had a high temperature. His arms and legs swelled rapidly, and he suffered intense pain. Two sailors went with him everywhere as bodyguards, to try to stop him falling and hurting himself. He dressed as a sailor in the Russian navy or wore a *Cossack* uniform with fur cap and long boots, and his parents bought him expensive toys – warships, trains and soldiers, and special uniforms – to take his attention away from rough, active games. The girls led his playful donkey Vanka or pulled Alexei on a sledge through the snow with his spaniel, Joy. They adored their young brother. His English and Swiss *tutors*, Sidney Gibbes and Pierre Gilliard, stopped him becoming spoilt through too much attention. They found Alexei a cheerful, good-humoured boy with a lively mind. Gilliard remembered his 'long, finely chiselled face, delicate features, auburn hair with a coppery glint in it, and large blue grey eyes like his mother's'.

The royal family spent little time in the beautiful Winter Palace in St Petersburg. The nobility were annoyed that they did not often go to the balls and receptions, or to the theatre

where Anna Pavlova danced in Swan Lake. Nicholas and Alexandra preferred to stay in their country house in the Crimea in the south of Russia, or remain at the summer palace at Tsarskoe Selo twenty-four kilometres outside the capital. Walking, boating, riding, sketching, reading, playing cards or chess were the things they most enjoyed. Though shy in public, Alexandra dominated her husband, but they were blissfully happy together and seemed perfectly content only in their own company. Nicholas had simple tastes even though he was Tsar of a huge empire.

Opposite: *The Tsar's children – left to right – Maria, Olga, Anastasia, Tatiana and the Tsarevich Alexei*

2 An English Girl's View of Russia

Hundreds of foreigners lived in Russia in the late nineteenth century. There were engineers, factory managers, businessmen and many English *governesses*. The governesses were employed by wealthy Russian families who spoke French, German and English, and wanted their children to speak English well. They got their jobs through a network of friends and had their own hostel in Moscow.

Miss Eager came to teach the Tsar's daughters. Rosamund Dowse, an energetic eighteen-year-old Norwich girl, worked for an army officer's family and for the governor of Samara. Emma Dashwood, also from Norwich, lived with the rich Rahl family. They let Emma and her friends use their box at the Bolshoi theatre, and took her to see Tchaikovsky's ballet 'The Sleeping Beauty'. Emma had never been to a ballet before she visited Russia, and was thrilled. Then there was the dashing red-haired governess, Edith Sinclair, who married a Russian naval officer, who was the son of an admiral. Actually she married him twice, once in Russia and once in England.

As well as teaching English, the governesses took their children on brisk walks every day. They gave them piano lessons, and regular cold baths, and insisted that toys must not be left untidily around but stored in a 'proper English Toy Cupboard'. One Russian mother was not sure what this was. 'Would the stables be suitable?' she asked Emma Dashwood. Emma said that a few shelves with glass doors in the nursery would do nicely.

The Russian children read Beatrix Potter's animal stories,

and annuals bought from the English shop in St Petersburg. Then they learnt English poetry, and read English novels such as 'Little Women' and the novels of Charles Dickens. They were told all about the English royal family, and the British empire. If Russian children learnt something about England, the English governesses learnt much more about Russia. Through their letters, diaries, clear memories and faded photographs we, too, can get a glimpse of Russian life.

The governesses travelled to Russia in various ways. Some went on the two-day train journey by Nord Express which cost £14. The train left Charing Cross station daily for Berlin and Poland. At the Polish frontier the passengers changed to a Russian train bound for St Petersburg or Moscow. Other girls sailed by cargo boat for £7 from Hull or London. They arrived in St Petersburg homesick, and often seasick, and found the northern city bitterly cold. Wealthy people, of course, could cruise to Russia in a ship, spending a month visiting Malta, Alexandria and Constantinople before calling at Odessa in southern Russia.

Perhaps our English governesses took with them Karl Baedeker's new guide book, which had splendid maps, and a great deal of helpful information about strange Russian customs. The girls would have to remember when writing home that 14 January in England was 1 January in Russia. Russia was still using the old Julian calendar which was thirteen days behind the Western Gregorian calendar. Baedeker advised travellers always to wear thick woollen underwear, and to take an air cushion and linen sheets (useful on long rail journeys and in small hotels), a small rubber bath, insect powder and, in Siberia, a revolver!

The governesses kept a wary eye on their luggage and NEVER sent it on in advance. They packed their things in plain paper, as Russian police were very suspicious of foreign newspapers. They took care their passports and *visa* papers were in order as it was illegal to travel in Russia without such papers. The police inspected them in towns, and they were sometimes needed when visiting museums and art galleries.

When the girls reached Russia, they could easily change their banknotes and *sovereigns* into Russian money. A silver *rouble* was worth about ten pence; five, ten and fifteen rouble pieces were gold coins. They also needed lots of *kopeks*, small copper coins, to tip cabmen and give to beggars.

The first things the governesses usually bought were well-lined rubber boots and warm furs. They wore a heavy winter coat called a shooba, and *galoshes* when the thaw began. Emma Dashwood had a beautiful white swansdown hood lined with white Jap silk which she wore over a fur turban she brought from England! Another early buy was usually Baedeker's cheap little '*Manual* of the Russian language'. You are lost in Russia and unable to read tram signs or street names, until you have mastered the different Russian alphabet.

What did our governesses notice most in Russia? First there was the delicious unusual food: little hot patties stuffed with fish roe or hard-boiled egg, sorrel soup, zakuska, which were mouth-watering savoury starters. There were wonderful ice-creams, game birds and sucking pigs served with cucumber and horse-radish sauce, pink fish like salmon from the river Volga, and cranberries with huge dishes of frothy sour cream. To drink they had tea (without milk), kvass which was a kind of home-brewed beer made from rye bread, and vodichka made from blackcurrant leaves, sultanas, lemons, sugar and water.

On the tables were thick white *damask* table cloths, and a lot of heavy silver. The English girls thought it delightful when the children kissed their parents, and thanked them, in French, for the meal afterwards. However they disapproved of the Russian custom of always leaving some food on the plate. If the servants saw the plates empty they thought you wanted a second helping.

Russian plumbing was different from that at home. Rosamund Dowse's employers, the Naumoffs, lived in Samara on the Volga. She had great difficulty in 'pedalling' the water so that it flowed from a tank above into the wash basin. There was no plug either, so you had to wash quickly before the water disappeared into the pail below. Samara had no proper sewage pipes, so the local *convicts* collected sewage from *septic* tanks in barrels on sledges and emptied it into the Volga river. The laundry maids did the monthly household wash in the river too. No wonder all drinking water was boiled in Russia!

Every summer the Naumoffs left Samara by steamer, travelling along the Volga to their country estate. Mr Naumoff was governor of the province so the family were always seen off with great ceremony by the chief commissioner of police. English governesses had very happy memories of Russian country life. The big wooden dachas (country houses) were painted a delicate pale blue, pink or green. Frogs croaked by the river and nightingales sang in lilac bushes in the garden. After morning lessons, the young people played tennis, went fishing or ordered the troikas (carriages) and went for a picnic. Occasionally there might be a dance with the officers when a regiment of soldiers passed that way.

In the country, governesses caught glimpses of peasants. There was class distinction in England of course, but the differences were greater in Russia. They sometimes saw a drunken peasant begging in the streets. They also discovered how immensely strong some Russian peasants were. When the Naumoffs travelled to the country they took twenty-two servants, three horses and a great quantity of luggage. Two sturdy Russian peasants slung the girls' piano on their backs, and cheerfully put it on the steamer. Like the Volga boatmen who hauled large barges along the river, they sang loudly. Peasant girls, too, thought nothing of working in the fields until the day their babies were born, and they returned to work the next day.

Most peasants soon lost their strength. Mary Brown remembered wretched peasants with their hollow-eyed, skinny children bringing wild strawberries from the woods to sell at the Big House. Later she went to the little village shop with Manya and Ira, the children she looked after, to spend their pocket money. A poor ragged woman there seized her hand and kissed it, weeping. 'Praise God for your goodness. Until

I got the money for the strawberries we had nothing to buy food with. Now we can have a good meal.' The English governess felt ashamed and sad. Manya and Ira were spending more money on sweets and biscuits than that poor woman's family had in a week.

The governesses travelled about a good deal. They noticed that Russian railway lines were wider than in the rest of Europe, and the trains usually burned wood, and travelled very slowly. The first-class carriages were blue, the second-class yellow, and the third-class green.

The first-class coaches were very comfortable, with stoves and restaurant cars, and attendants who provided bedding. Second- and third-class passengers took with them masses of cushions, kettles, and awkward packages. Long stops were made at stations when everyone got off and bought food from waiters in white aprons on the platform. Tea was sold all day and night, at ten kopeks a glass, or passengers filled their own kettles from a huge copper saucepan of boiling water. Little barefoot peasant children offered lilies of the valley, onions and cucumbers for sale. Fifteen minutes before leaving, a bell was rung, and a second bell ten minutes later. Finally a third bell sounded and the train steamed off. The head guard looked very important with his round fur cap, masses of silver and red braid, black blouse and wide trousers tucked into black boots. Many people seemed to wear uniforms in Russia – not only soldiers, but students, children and countless officials too.

THE GREAT SIBERIAN RAILWAY
Rosamund Dowse travelled on Russia's most exciting railway, the Trans-Siberian railway (T.S.R). She remembered the dusty lines and platforms of rough earth and, though all the train windows had double panes and were shut, she had to wipe the dust continually off her face.

Opposite: *Travelling on the Trans-Siberian Railway. Passengers stopped at stations to buy fruit and tea (left)*

Nicholas II's father and grandfather had dreamed of a great railway, the longest in the world, to link St Petersburg with Russia's Pacific coast. Peasants hungry for land would be able to travel by train, and settle in farms by the railway line. Huge deposits of gold, iron and other minerals, which surveys showed were lying waste in Siberia, could be mined. And if Russia's expansion eastwards led to war with neighbouring Japan or China, soldiers could be rapidly transported to the front. The whole venture would show that Russia was becoming a great industrial power.

Nicholas's father commanded: 'Your Imperial Highness is to lay the first stone at Vladivostok.' So in May 1891 Nicholas travelled by steamer to the little Russian port in the Pacific. He filled a wheelbarrow with earth and laid it on the first bit of railway line. When he became Tsar in 1894, Nicholas also became president of the committee building the railway. He declared that he hoped to complete quickly, cheaply and solidly 'this peaceful work, entrusted to me by my beloved father'.

The state provided the money and the line was nearly finished between 1892 and 1898. Russian engineers made surveys, and constructed great steel bridges over mighty rivers like the Tobol, Ob and Tom. They were very long, and expensive to build, as they had to rest on huge stone piles capable of resisting the shock of enormous masses of floating ice. Large new steamers linked the railway with river traffic.

Most of the land was very flat. One French traveller could not recall passing through a tunnel for hundreds of kilometres, but around the very deep Lake Baikal the line wound in deep zigzags in great valleys in the mountains. The train was carried across the lake by a large icebreaking steamer built by a British firm.

Thousands of strong peasants built the railway line. Peasants were used to leaving their wives and belongings at home, and trudging hundreds of miles in search of work. They worked hard throughout the short summers, and during the seven months of severe frost and snow in the Siberian winters they huddled snowbound in their wooden cabins, mostly sleeping and drinking *vodka*.

The government hoped to encourage foreign businessmen to use the railway and published in 1900 a huge 'Guide to the Great Siberian Railway'. They stressed it was cheaper, and twice as quick as going east by sea, through the Suez canal. It took a month travelling from London to Shanghai in China by boat, but less than a fortnight by the T.S.R. A branch line was built through Manchuria, a Chinese province, to Port Arthur, to encourage trade with China and Japan.

Many kinds of people, including English governesses, used the T.S.R. *Diplomats* and important businessmen travelled first-class. Miners and engineers, *emigrant* peasants and their families, animals and bundles, crowded on to the wooden benches of the third-class coaches. The government charged settlers to Siberia reduced fares and lent them money to develop farms along the line and to buy seed corn and timber for houses.

In many towns along the route, Nicholas provided centres where the peasants could get hot food and medical attention at very low cost. There were stores where they could buy cheap furniture and utensils. As the clergy only visited such remote areas once or twice a year, there were very few churches in Siberia, so in 1894 Nicholas started a public subscription to build churches, and schools, at every railway station along the T.S.R. in memory of his father.

Usually the governesses found Russian provincial towns rather uninteresting. They were all much alike, laid out in a square, with broad, badly paved roads, often without any pavement. The churches had onion-shaped domes, usually painted silver, gold or blue. Most of the houses were wooden although a few important ones were made of stone. Old men in cabs, called droshkies, or sleighs in winter, collected travellers from the railway station. There might be a museum or library, but not often a park, and the English girls thought the shops were dreadful compared with those at home.

Of course they enjoyed exploring St Petersburg and Moscow. St Petersburg, with its wide streets, canals, fine churches, and

splendid palaces owned by the nobles, was a beautiful city. They might drive down the fashionable Nevsky Prospekt, St Petersburg's leading street, past expensive shops. Or they might skim along the frozen river Neva by sledge in winter. St Petersburg had wonderful theatres, concert halls, gardens and public galleries. Every week the Tsar opened his splendid collection of pictures at the Winter Palace to the public. The English girls saw nothing of life in the slums where the industrial workers lived.

Moscow was a stranger, more Eastern city, less regularly planned, and less fashionable than St Petersburg. However, the Moscow Art Theatre was renowned and everybody was talking about Anton Chekhov's new plays 'The Cherry Orchard' and 'The Seagull'.

Rosamund Dowse, like countless other visitors, was thrilled by her visit to the Kremlin – the huge red-walled fortress in the centre of Moscow. Its buildings included splendid gold and white cathedrals, and she saw the large, broken Tsar's bell, so big that a horse and cart could be driven through it. She admired the breathtakingly beautiful *icons*, jewels and treasures which the Tsar stored in the Kremlin.

Some of the governesses may have gone with their rich families to buy expensive presents at Fabergé's jewellery shop. He made exquisite little pill-boxes, clocks, brooches, photo frames, and, above all, jewelled Easter eggs. The royal family and nobles gave them to their friends at Easter time. When pressed open, they contained delightful little presents. One of the most beautiful was a little golden egg only twelve centimetres high, decorated with diamonds and tiny black imperial eagles. It was given by Nicholas II to Alexandra. Inside, the 'surprise' was a beautiful model of their golden coronation coach, only seven centimetres long but perfect in every detail, with rock crystal windows, blue enamel curtains, doors which opened, and two steps which let down.

Opposite: *The river Neva at St Petersburg*

Moscow, a city of domed churches and cobbled streets choked with horse-drawn vehicles

Buying Fabergé's expensive and elegant knick-knacks ended in 1917. When the revolution broke out most of the English governesses sadly left Russia, leaving behind the kind families they loved, and many of the hard-earned roubles they had saved. A few regarded Russia as their real home and continued to live there.

In 1916 one governess noticed that the peasants glowered in a frightening way, and shouted abuse, as the noble family swept along in their carriage to a picnic in the country. Others remembered seeing their employers hiding their jewels in corners of the grounds, away from the prying eyes of their peasant servants.

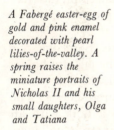

A Fabergé easter-egg of gold and pink enamel decorated with pearl lilies-of-the-valley. A spring raises the miniature portraits of Nicholas II and his small daughters, Olga and Tatiana

Rosamund Dowse was in St Petersburg in 1917. Queues for bread were becoming longer. There were soldiers in the streets, and occasional gun firing. She squeezed one day on to a crowded tram, clinging to the outside with the help of two strong peasant soldiers. When she got ready to pay her fare, they laughed and said she need not bother 'now we have freedom'. Rosamund insisted, firmly: 'I am English, and we are free, but we still pay our fares on buses and trams.'

3 Village Life

Spring arrived suddenly. The winding road through the village was ankle-deep in mud and slush. Icefloes cracked on the river, flocks of wild duck took wing over water meadows, a *crane* settled on the tallest tree in the birch copse.

There had been a fire the night before. Someone had carelessly overturned the *samovar* and one of the peasant houses lay in charred ruins. Everyone scurried to fill water pails, and rushed outside with sheepskins and treasured chests. The simple village fire engine, little more than a tank with an ancient hosepipe, creaked away. Three or four strong villagers started trimming wood with axes. The family would have a new home within the week.

The peasant houses, called isbas, were built on oblong plots on either side of the unpaved road. They were built of stout wooden logs made watertight by stuffing the cracks with moss. Each isba had a steep roof and elaborately carved woodwork on window shutters and door. Further south, where timber was scarce, houses had straw roofs. In the treeless *steppe* they were of beaten clay, plastered on a *wattle* frame and whitewashed.

Children, grandparents, aunts and uncles all lived together in one room. Below was a cellar for storing grain, and for animals. The baby, tightly *swaddled*, swung in a cradle from the open rafters of the smoky roof. Grandmother cooked meals and baked black rye bread on the huge brick stove. It was cool in summer, and warm from the fire in winter. Lucky members of the family slept at night on top, the rest covered themselves with sheepskin rugs and slept on broad, wooden benches which

A church and village school built by the great Russian writer, Turgeniev

stretched round the walls. Some of the girls had to make do with straw in huts in the yard.

There was little furniture – a home-made table, pots, ladles, wooden washtubs, and, prized possession, a copper samovar for boiling tea. The walls were decorated with pictures of favourite saints like St George fighting the dragon, and photos of the Tsar and his family, cut out of old magazines. A tiny lamp flickered on a small shelf before a wooden painted icon of St Nicholas in one corner. Everyone crossed himself in front of the icon on entering the house, and said a quick prayer before it at night, to protect the family from evil spirits. Sometimes they had a tattered old Bible on the shelf too, but few peasants could read it and anyway the cottage was always too dark. Paraffin lamps and matches were luxuries, and at night 25 many households still only had a flickering light of burning wood.

A Russian peasant using a primitive plough

During the five or six months farming season, the whole family toiled for eighteen hours a day. The village was their world and their work was organised, as it had been for centuries, according to the rhythm of the seasons. They knew little of towns, and nothing of countries beyond it. Around the village lay three great open fields stretching for miles. Each was divided into long, narrow, hedgeless strips about three or four metres wide, and several metres long. Every family owned twenty or thirty strips scattered over the fields.

The men scratched the soil with a simple wheel-less plough dragged by one lean horse. It did not plough deeply, but needed little effort. In May one field was sowed with oats and another field would be sown with winter rye in August. The third field remained fallow or resting. Next year they would vary the crops on the fields so that the fallow field grew corn and one of the others rested.

In June they all went to the lime grove and carefully cut lime bark. The first layer was useful for roofing houses, the

Russian peasants eating their mid-day meal in the hayfield. Notice the plaited sandals (lapti) on their feet

second, soaked throughout the summer, and dried in winter, was cut into strips and plaited into rough sandals called lapti. Everyone wore out several pairs each month. At the end of June, they scythed the lush waist-high grass in the meadows, and then reaped the corn with sickles. Men, women and children all took part in the harvesting. The girls built tents to provide shade in the fields from the scorching sun. The babies, still tightly swaddled, hung in little hammocks slung from three sticks stuck in the ground. If the villagers were lucky, and there had been no disastrous drought in spring or heavy rains in summer, they might harvest five times the corn they had sown. Most European countries got a tenfold return, but with a severe climate, little manure, and hardly any modern machinery, Russia had the lowest yield in Europe.

In summer the gentry came from town to spend a few months in the country. The big houses were opened up and the villagers caught glimpses of families going for picnics in their carriages. The peasants picked wild strawberries in the woods. The boys made simple traps and caught birds and rabbits, fished in the river, and collected honey from wild bees in the forest. The road through the village became dusty, with hard, deep ruts made by passing farm carts. Scraggy chickens and white geese scratched for oats by the miller's house. Grandma drove them off her dusty cabbages with a willow switch, and stood admiring her huge sunflowers by the fence. In winter she used the oil from their seeds for cooking. Cattle grazed in the green water meadows and the laughter of girls washing clothes in the river echoed through the village.

In August and September the peasants sowed winter rye, cut firewood from the forest and dried mushrooms on strings. Then the first flurries of snow appeared in October. Soon there would be deep drifts and the peasants would be house-bound for six months. The older folk mostly spent their time asleep on the stove, while some of the young people travelled to the nearest town by sledge to find odd jobs as waiters, sleigh drivers or factory workers. The rest worked at their cottage crafts, making toys and *accordions*, carving wooden spoons and bowls, spinning, weaving and painting icons. Travelling merchants bought their products each spring for a few roubles. Older folk grumbled that the profits were smaller now that mass-produced goods could be turned out more cheaply in the factories.

AMUSEMENTS

Sometimes there was a rest from toil. The travelling *pedlar*, in his old-fashioned black trousers and peaked cap, brought excitement and news from neighbouring villages. He was a welcome visitor with his bagful of trinkets – cheap icons, ribbons, needles and scissors.

The weekly market and fairs were held in summer. Travelling traders with carts set up stalls in the broad village street and sold cheap cotton cloth, matches and paraffin lamps, new samovars, salt, tea and sugar – all the little luxuries that villages could not produce themselves. There were horses and cattle for sale too.

The peasants made baggy trousers from their own sheep's wool and wove homely linen shirts from their own flax and hemp. They plaited crude sandals from bark and made white felt boots for winter. Then the men wore furry caps and a long trench coat of coarse material, or sheepskin coats smelling of sweat, oil and rotten food. The women wore coloured head scarves, homespun blouses and long skirts, with thick cloaks in winter. At festival times the best clothes came out of the family chest. The boys had brightly coloured shirts and polished boots, which they sometimes carefully removed before walking through mud. The girls wore fancy sleeveless slips called sarafans, and ornamental head-dresses like tiaras, covered with artificial pearls, ribbons and glass beads. There was gay dancing to the music of accordions and *balalaikas*, and the young men pushed the girls higher and higher on the village swing.

The older men spent a lot of time at the local inn. It looked just like a peasant's cottage, except for its red-checked curtains and rather dirty table cloths. Here you could gossip, eat salted cucumbers, onions and black rye bread, and above all drink – bottles of vodka, or glass after glass of hot tea – till you sweated. There was an old saying that a real *booze* took three days, one to drink, one to be drunk, and the third day to sober up.

Christenings, funerals and weddings were special occasions for drinking. Marriages were arranged by the village match-maker who visited both families. When the groom's father had decided with the bride's father that the *dowry* was enough, they wrapped their hands in a coat and shook them as a sign that the engagement was completed. At the church, pages held crowns over the heads of the bride and groom, who carried candles. It was a common belief that the one whose candle burnt longest would outlive the other. Then the bearded priest gave each a wedding ring, they kissed, drank wine from the same glass, and followed him three times round the church with their hands tied together. After this the wife had a hard life bringing up her large family. Her husband beat her regularly, but she accepted it without complaint, perhaps as a sign that he still took some interest in her!

The church insisted on many days of fasting, when no one could eat meat or drink milk. Wednesdays and Fridays were fast days, and also the forty days of Lent before Easter. There were numerous festival days too – the feasts of St Nicholas in May and December, the carnival before Lent, and holy days at Easter and Christmas. Then the priest organised religious processions through the village. Holy icons were carried and blessed, sheep killed and eaten, and lots of vodka drunk. Chekhov describes one such feast in a short story: one peasant got terribly drunk for three days. He drank the cap off his head and the boots off his feet, and beat Marya, his poor wife, so hard she had to be cooled down with water. Later everyone felt ashamed, and very sick.

CHURCH AND VILLAGE ASSEMBLY

Most peasants had not read the Bible, and many were frightened of evil spirits. But on Sundays and procession days they had glimpses of a splendid, comforting world. They entered the dark wooden church, dimly lit by candles, and queued up to confess their sins to the priest. They kissed the cross and the Bible, and gave their names to the *deacon* who kept a list. They stood for a long time gazing at the great screen, the *iconostasis*, which separated them from the holiest part of the church. Here dozens of little lamps glowed before scores of blackened icons in gilded frames. The priest, in elaborate robes, chanted loudly in the old *Slavonic* tongue. Then he gave each peasant a spoonful of holy wine in which a little piece of holy bread had been dipped. Afterwards the beautiful singing from the choirboys continued.

The villagers often laughed at their priest when he got tipsy with vodka like the rest, yet he was at the centre of their lives when they married, fell ill or lay dying. He blessed the young men going off to army service and carried holy icons to bless the harvest. At Easter there was a special feeling of celebration

Opposite: *Inside a Russian church. The richly decorated screen is covered with holy pictures, or icons*

and oneness in the village as everyone kissed each other, and uttered the familiar words, 'Christ has risen, in truth he has risen'.

On Sundays, after church, men who were head of each household met in the *mir*, the village assembly. Every three years they elected a village *elder* to be in charge of meetings and keep order. He wore a bronze badge on a chain round his neck. The mir discussed which village boys should serve in the army, and how they would share out strips in the open fields. This was done about every twenty years, as some families became larger and needed more land. Family quarrels were settled, and passports issued, allowing individuals to leave the village and work in the towns. The mir insisted they sent money home regularly. Many villagers were still paying off the *redemption taxes* to the government every year for land gained in *emancipation*. They saved very little, and often borrowed from the miller, who lent money as well as grinding corn. Others would rather borrow from the new Peasant Bank which charged less *interest*. If anyone got behind with his taxes, the village elder would *confiscate* his hens or his samovar, and perhaps call in the local police inspector. The mir was also held responsible for the behaviour of its peasants.

Peasants were taught by priests that the Tsar had been created by God to take care of them, and give them orders. Perhaps one day he would give them more land. Meanwhile most accepted their hard life, and dared not hope for better things. As an old Russian proverb said, 'God is too high, and the Tsar too far away'.

4 The Tsar's Problems

Nicholas II's stern father had simple tastes and expected his son to sleep on a hard bed and get up at seven. He taught Nicholas to respect him, to fear God, to do his duty and to be brave. Nicholas's sister said he was trained only as a soldier. 'He should have been taught *statesmanship* and he was not.' Nicholas did not really want to be Tsar, and would probably have preferred to live an outdoor life as a country gentleman. He was good-tempered and kind, charming and dignified. But although he worked hard and conscientiously, he was weak as a ruler. He lacked the judgment to choose good ministers. He was also stubborn and not prepared to move with the times and try new ways of ruling Russia. Alexandra influenced him too much. She told the British ambassador, 'The Emperor unfortunately is weak, but I am not, and intend to be firm.'

Alexander III expected his son to rule like earlier Tsars, as an autocrat – one who does not share his power. So, when he became Tsar Nicholas declared, 'Let all know that in devoting all my strength on behalf of the welfare of my people I shall defend the principles of *autocracy* as unswervingly as my dead father.' He felt he was responsible to God alone for his actions. Russia had no parliament until he unwillingly allowed the first one to meet in 1906. There were many demands for a share in government, especially from the educated people such as lawyers, doctors, university teachers and the few businessmen in the Empire. But the Tsar always chose and dismissed his ministers.

The most important minister, the Minister of the Interior, supervised the governors of the Empire's ninety-six provinces.

He kept order, and dealt with the police and postal services. The Tsar controlled the army and navy, issued laws, and raised taxes. He supervised the press and universities.

He had a powerful secret police called the Okhrana with agents everywhere, disguised as servants, newspaper sellers or coachmen. They kept an eye on towns and villages, factories and railways. The Okhrana collected detailed information about troublemakers, and kept names of revolutionaries. They examined letters and parcels. It was said that even Nicholas's mother, the Dowager Empress, might find her correspondence opened by them.

Nicholas could always count on the support of his wealthy relatives, grand dukes and grand duchesses, uncles and cousins, who owned large estates throughout the country. There was also a large class of noblemen. Few of them took any share in government, but Nicholas knew they would help him in discouraging changes. He was also helped by loyal clergy of the Russian Orthodox church who taught the people to be obedient to the Tsar. The clergy were controlled by the state, and Nicholas appointed the archbishops and bishops. The churches, with their onion-shaped domes painted blue, green or gold, were an important feature of every town and village. The clergy controlled most of the schools and colleges in the country, and their many church festivals played an important part in people's lives. But as the Empire expanded, it included numbers of Catholics, Protestants, Jews and Muslims. These people had little freedom, and they resented the special position of the Orthodox church.

One of Nicholas's problems, shared by other Russian rulers, was the enormous size of the Empire (see the map on page 5) 'Russia is not a country, it is a world', runs an old peasant proverb. The Tsar's lands covered one-seventh of the earth's surface, and stretched from the Baltic sea to the Pacific, and from the frozen Arctic to the Black sea and the borders of Persia, China and Mongolia. They had every variety of climate and scenery – enormous lakes, broad rivers like the Volga and Ob, high mountain ranges, dense, gloomy forests of fir and pine, and immense, treeless plains of rich black earth (the steppe). Most travellers only knew the more thickly populated European areas, but beyond the Ural mountains there was Siberia, the Asian part of the Empire. In its enormous open expanses you could travel for hours without seeing anyone.

In Siberia enterprising peasants battled against harsh extremes of heat and cold on their isolated farms. Revolutionaries were sent into exile there, and convicts were sentenced to hard labour in the mines and quarries.

There were 130 million people in Russia in 1897, nearly as many as in England, France and Germany combined. In the eighteenth and nineteenth centuries the Empire conquered neighbouring people so that it came to include more than eighty different nationalities: as well as Russians, there were Poles, Finns, Germans, Tartars, Ukrainians, Georgians, Armenians and many others. Non-Russians made up nearly half of the people in the Empire. They were unhappy and restless at being so firmly controlled from St Petersburg, and proud of their old customs and traditions; they wanted books and newspapers in their own languages, and more say in running their affairs.

Five million Jews lived in Poland and an area east of Poland called the Pale. Jews had special grievances: they could not join the navy or some regiments, or get work as lawyers or local officials. They could not go to certain universities, and were not allowed to buy land outside cities. Sometimes Jews were treated savagely, and had to flee from their homes to escape being murdered. Nicholas should have done much more to please all these different peoples, but he tended to accept things as they were, rather than to act boldly to change them. 'Whatever I do, nothing succeeds. I am out of luck,' he once said sadly.

Four out of five Russians were poor, backward peasants, and these were another of Nicholas's problems. Before his grandfather Alexander II had freed them in 1861, many peasants were serfs who had to work for their masters without pay, could be separated from their families and sold, flogged by their owners, or sent to serve in the army for twenty-five 35

years. After 1861 they received wages, and were also given some of the landlords' land which was shared out in strips by their village assembly, the mir. The government paid the landlords for the land, and the peasants would have to pay the government a redemption tax over forty-nine years.

Though the freeing of the serfs helped them, it did not solve Russia's farming problems. Landlords still kept a lot of land, especially meadow and woodland, but took little interest in developing their estates, and few spent money on fertilisers or up-to-date machinery. There were frequent quarrels about firewood and pasturing animals. Peasants, of course, had no money to spare from their redemption payments and were often deep in debt. *Illiterate* and backward, they could not understand the value of new farming methods or the use of machinery. A Scottish engineer who brought some of the first threshing and reaping machines to south Russia remembered how 'they took off their caps and crossed themselves, praying devoutly that they might not be present at some invention of the devil'. There was also a shortage of land as the peasant population greatly increased in the nineteenth century, so some of them drifted to towns to find work in factories. Others went to Siberia.

Nicholas liked to think of the peasants as loyal to him, but often in the past they had been rebellious. The hardships of his time made them more so. In 1905, a year of revolution, villagers burnt landlords' houses, and seized some of their land. In 1906 Nicholas's minister ordered changes, hoping to win over some of the more ambitious peasants to support the government. He allowed keen peasants to run individual farms if they wished, instead of farming jointly, and he abolished redemption payments. Some peasants were given money to settle in Siberia. But by 1917, the year of Russia's great revolution, the peasants had lost all confidence in help from the Tsar. They looted and burned the landlords' crops, and

Opposite: *Food being distributed to poor villagers during a famine. Notice the rough wooden houses with roofs made of turf*

were ready to support anyone who seemed likely to give them land.

Many of the town workers were little better-off than the peasants. The population was increasing, and Russia was rapidly becoming a great industrial country, facing many of the problems England had faced a century earlier. Dangerous factory machinery was not protected. Trade unions were forbidden. Workers often toiled for thirteen or fourteen hours a day, although Nicholas had issued a law in 1897 to shorten working hours. A typical factory inspector's report described how 'the workers, all in greasy, soot-covered rags, covered with a thick layer of grime and dust, swarm like bees in extremely dirty and *congested* quarters'.

Huge barracks built by the employers contained over-crowded dormitories where twenty or thirty men slept. As the men worked in shifts, the beds were seldom empty. Workers with families had tiny, smelly cubicles, divided by old canvas hangings; if they were lucky, they had bunk beds and a table and chair. Lines of washing and babies in cradles hung from the ceilings. The air was steamy from the smoky stove in the corner where everyone did their cooking.

Many of the factories were very large and owned by the government. Others had foreign managers, and had been built with foreigners' money. The workers often felt little loyalty to their employers and so it was easy for revolutionaries to organise demonstrations and illegal strikes among the large masses of discontented people.

Opposite: *Moscow washerwomen at work in a bitterly cold laundry. Their loads are dragged across the ice on wooden sledges*

5 Russian Revolutionaries

Revolutionaries had been active in Russia for so long that Nicholas, like everyone else, accepted them as part of life. Russia lacked the means of expressing discontent which many other countries had. There were no newspapers which were not controlled by the government, and no parliament. Trade unions were forbidden, demonstrations and strikes were illegal. Even people who made mild criticisms of the government might be arrested as troublemakers by the secret police. Although some Tsars allowed freedom for a while, they usually treated people harshly again a few years later, so many Russians felt forced to become revolutionaries, attempting to overthrow the government by violence.

The heroes most admired by revolutionaries of Nicholas's time were the Decembrists, a group of young army officers who tried to kill Tsar Nicholas I in December 1825. Taking their ideas from revolutionary leaders in France, they wanted a parliament, the end of serfdom, and freedom of speech, writing and religion. More than 120 were seized and brought to trial. Some were hanged, others sent to harsh labour camps in Siberia, where for many years they kept in touch with other revolutionaries. Today a great square in St Petersburg (Leningrad) is called Decembrist Square after them.

Under Nicholas's father and grandfather new revolutionary groups became active, with stirring names like 'Land and Liberty' and 'The People's Will'. Many of their leaders spent long periods exiled abroad, often in Switzerland. They smuggled revolutionary pamphlets back into Russia.

Students were their keenest supporters. They had little money and poor lodgings, and were often expelled from college for organising demonstrations or not paying their fees. They bitterly resented the lack of freedom at universities, and sympathised with downtrodden peasants and workers. Those who had studied chemistry made homemade bombs to blow up buildings, or to murder policemen or officials. (One such student was Lenin's brother Alexander.)

Many called themselves the Narodniki or populists. Their slogan was 'To the people'. Hoping to stir up revolution among the peasants, they joined wandering labourers at harvest time, and dressed and lived like peasants. But though keen and energetic, they knew little of real peasant life. The villagers were suspicious of these town strangers, and could not understand their revolutionary pamphlets and ideas. Most peasants still remained loyal to the Tsar. The police dealt quickly with the *amateurish* troublemakers.

Under Nicholas II the revolutionaries became more ruthless and better organised. A group called the Socialist Revolutionaries carried out acts of terror, and brutally murdered leading officials and ministers. Among their victims were the Tsar's brother-in-law, and the Minister of the Interior, Plehve, who was killed by a bomb in St Petersburg. Another minister, Peter Stolypin, was shot in 1911 while watching an opera in Kiev with the royal family. 'The Emperor standing in the front of his box looked worried and sad, but showed no sign of fear.' 'Supported by friends, Stolypin managed to walk out of the theatre, a brave effort which earned him a tremendous *ovation*.' He died five days later. Members of the Romanov family were in constant danger and had always to be closely guarded. Whenever the Tsar travelled by train, two identical blue trains with royal coats of arms made the journey. No one ever knew which contained the royal family.

The newest group of revolutionaries were the *Bolsheviks* or *communists*, who had split from the movement of trade unionists and socialists who called themselves *Social Democrats*. The Bolsheviks regarded the murder of individuals as a waste of

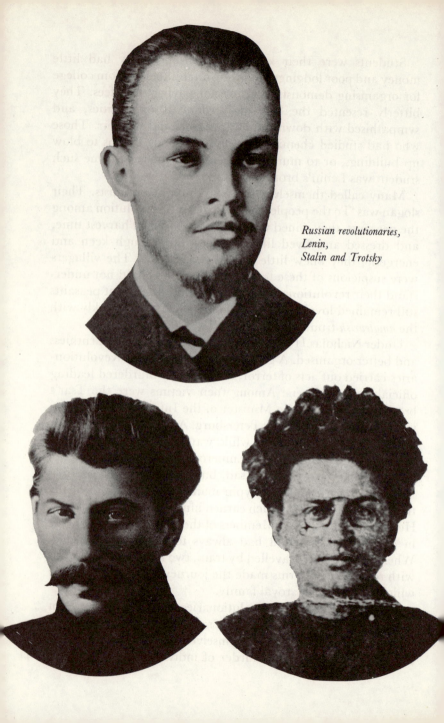

*Russian revolutionaries,
Lenin,
Stalin and Trotsky*

time, and aimed to overthrow the whole system of Russian government by organising an armed rebellion of town workers rather than peasants. They formed secret committees or 'cells' among factory workers, dockers and railwaymen. They believed that such people, if properly organised, could demonstrate and strike in the big cities and bring Russia's trade, railways and industry to a standstill. They had taken these ideas from the writings of the German, Karl Marx, who taught that the time would come when the working people would be strong enough to overthrow the owners of property.

The Bolshevik leaders, Lenin, Trotsky and Stalin, were ruthless, clever men toughened by years of exile abroad and in Siberia. They had money, often seized in daring bank raids, and wrote stirring newspapers like 'The Spark' (Iskra) and 'Truth' (Pravda). These were published abroad and smuggled into Russia through a network of followers. Above all, the Bolsheviks had very clear ideas about how to carry out a full-scale revolution when the time was ripe. This happened in 1917, but only after the Tsar's government had already been overthrown.

Nicholas's police imprisoned anyone suspected of being a trouble-maker in prisons like the Peter and Paul fortress, a huge, dreary building opposite the Winter Palace across the river Neva. Here in miserable, dank cells with tiny windows, stone floors and hard iron beds, they spent weary years. Many died as a result of damp and poor food during their long imprisonment. Their cells are now open to the public, and the revolutionaries, whose photographs hang outside, are regarded as heroes.

Many strike leaders and revolutionaries joined the thieves and other criminals who were exiled to the desolate wastes of distant Siberia. Straggling lines of unfortunate men, with half-shaved heads and grey convict overcoats, could be seen trudging along. Their legs were raw from the jingling chains around them. Cossack troops in dark green uniforms closely guarded them with rifles. In the rear were creaking wagons, crowded with old people and ragged, half-starved children, 43

since convicts' families often went with them. After days of travelling on foot or by cart, and being packed into stinking river barges, the convicts reached the mines and labour camps. Here they would spend their remaining days in hard labour. Every spring, when the buds burst and the cuckoo sang, thousands escaped to freedom in the woods and mountains. They lived on roots and berries until the terrible Siberian winter came. Then they were easily recaptured.

Russian revolutionaries exiled in Siberia were usually treated better than convicts. Their chief punishment was not being allowed to return to great cities like St Petersburg and Moscow. Lenin, Stalin and Trotsky all spent time in Siberia, where they lived in simple huts with peasant families, were allowed to write letters and read library books, and could be sent money. Lenin enjoyed writing books, playing chess, hunting and skating. He married his wife Krupskaya, a fellow revolutionary, while in Siberia, and spent his time writing books about the great changes that he thought were about to take place in Russia.

6 War with Japan and Bloody Sunday

The Russo-Japanese War, 1904–5

Russian expansion in the Far East brought rivalry with Japan. By the early twentieth century Japan had developed into the most advanced country in Asia. Like Russia she wanted trade and colonies in Korea and Manchuria. These areas belonged to the Chinese empire which had a weak government unable to defend itself against powerful enemies. Russia had built a branch line of the T.S.R in Manchuria to Port Arthur (see the map opposite), a more useful port than Vladivostok because the sea there did not freeze in winter. Russians had also been granted rights by the Chinese to build railways and develop coalmines. They tended to despise the Japanese 'island dwarfs'. One Russian said, 'We'll pin one of these harmless butterflies on a postcard, and send him home as a souvenir.' When it came to war, the Russians were sure they would win. They thought their officers were superior, and could call up three million soldiers. They had a fine navy too, at Port Arthur. A war to drive the Japanese out of the disputed areas would be short and successful. 'One flag and one sentinel – the *prestige* of Russia will do the rest.'

The Tsar personally reviewed his troops and sailors at St Petersburg and Odessa to encourage them, but the ordinary people did not really understand why Russia was at war with Japan. The soldiers did not care about gaining land in Manchuria. As one remarked, 'We should not like to live here if it was given to us. As we travelled through Siberia we saw a lot of land. There is no end to it.'

However, eager to use their modern weapons, in 1904 the Japanese struck first. The brilliant Japanese admiral Togo completely surprised and destroyed the Russian fleet at Port Arthur and in January 1905 the Japanese captured the city. A month later Russian soldiers were disastrously defeated at Mukden, the Manchurian capital (see the map opposite), in a great battle lasting a fortnight. Weapons and desperately needed medical supplies were short, as the uncompleted T.S.R could only carry four troop trains a day. The Japanese had a big advantage in that they were fighting nearer home.   47

A Russian commander reported to the government that one of his surgeons had treated 12,000 men with the *index finger* blown off their right hand. Considering their fingers were well protected when firing, it seemed odd. Then he remembered a military rule that said a man was freed from service if he had lost a finger. Hundreds of peasants had *maimed* themselves intentionally in the hope of returning home. Revolutionary pamphlets were spreading among the troops too.

As the hardships of the fighting became known, members of the *zemstvos*, a kind of local county council established in many parts of Russia by Nicholas's grandfather Alexander II, joined together and offered to help the war effort by aiding wounded soldiers and their families. They ran hospitals, schools and libraries, and were the only means people had of sharing in Russian government. The zemstvos were distrusted by the Tsar's ministers who objected to their claims to run local affairs. The unpopular minister of the interior, Plehve, refused to accept their offer to help in the war.

In July 1904 the 'Daily Telegraph' correspondent happened to see two men on bicycles passing Plehve's carriage in St Petersburg. There was a deafening explosion like thunder, and broken glass tinkled on the pavement. He glimpsed a dead horse, pools of blood, fragments of carriage, a large hole in the ground. His own driver, convinced that the end of the world had come, was on his knees praying devoutly. Plehve had been killed by a bomb thrown by a revolutionary student. The journalist met no one who regretted Plehve's death, or condemned the *outrage*.

Meanwhile the war continued. There was a Russian fleet in the Black Sea, but its crews were unreliable, so the Russians decided to send their Baltic fleet to fight the Japanese. The amazing voyage through the English channel and round Africa and India lasted eight months. In the North Sea the Russian commander fired on some peaceful English fishing vessels, mistaking them for Japanese ships. This caused great fury in England.

The fleet sailed round the Cape of Good Hope and finally

met the Japanese fleet in the Straits of Tsushima, between Japan and Korea, in April 1905. The Japanese Admiral Togo, a great admirer of Admiral Nelson, signalled to his ships, 'The fate of the nation rests on this single battle. Let every man do his utmost.'

The Russians had more long-range guns, but the Japanese guns were quicker and more accurate. In less than an hour, tiny Japan had defeated the world's biggest nation in one of the greatest naval battles in history. A young Japanese boy watched it from a high pine tree on a neighbouring island. 'I never thought that warships looked so beautiful in the midst of a battle. As the shells fell into the sea they turned into hundreds of water columns. The guns flashed like lightning, and roared like a thousand thunderstorms.' Of some fifty fine Russian ships, only a couple of light cruisers and two destroyers finally limped into Vladivostok. Japanese losses were only 117 dead. But there were 5,000 Russians killed and 6,000 were taken prisoner. A peace conference was arranged by the American president Theodore Roosevelt. The *treaty* ending the war was signed at Portsmouth, New Hampshire, in September 1905. Thanks to the skilful bargaining of Russia's minister Witte, the terms were less humiliating than Russia deserved. She lost Port Arthur and southern Manchuria to Japan. Japan also had half of Sakhalin island, which Russia had used as a convict settlement, and a little later she occupied Korea. Russia had suffered a tremendous blow to her eastern expansion by being defeated by Japan. Even worse, these disasters sparked off revolution at home.

BLOODY SUNDAY

Russians realised the war against Japan was going badly when news reached St Petersburg that Port Arthur had fallen. Then in January 1905, after the dismissal of four men, trouble developed among the 13,000 workers at the important Putilov iron works in St Petersburg. They were supported by Father Gapon, a hardworking priest who sympathised with industrial workers and wanted to improve their conditions. He suggested   49

that the workers should ask their employers for an eight-hour working day, a daily wage increase to one rouble, and free medical aid. Other workers, including shipbuilders, and dockers, came out on strike too, and soon 25,000 men were idle.

Since the employers did nothing, Gapon decided to ask the Tsar to pass reforms. He firmly believed that Nicholas was being led astray by selfish officials and employers. If the 'Little Father' only knew of their situation, he would do something. Nicholas was making one of his rare visits to the capital to attend the archbishop's annual blessing of the water of the river Neva. Thousands thronged the streets to glimpse their Tsar on this public holiday.

Gapon collected a *petition* signed by workmen asking for reforms. (Many of them being unable to write made a cross.) They asked for a parliament, freedom of speech and religion, an eight-hour working day, the right to form trade unions, and an end to the Japanese war. Gapon expected thousands of other strikers in textile mills, furniture factories, breweries and chemical works would support him. He was loyal to the Tsar, and told the government openly that he was organising a peaceful demonstration march of workers and their families to present their petition to Nicholas at the Winter Palace.

Sunday 9 January 1905 (by the Russian calendar), later known as Bloody Sunday, dawned a cold, grey, raw day. A biting wind blew light flurries of snow. Led by Father Gapon, men, women and children approached Palace Square outside the palace, carrying icons, flags and portraits of the Tsar and Tsarina. Many sang their favourite hymns, and the police cleared the way as they always did for religious processions.

Meanwhile the new Minister of the Interior had decided that such protest marches were illegal, and must be stopped, by force if necessary. He ordered the police and Cossack troops to get ready. Twenty thousand soldiers spent the morning

Opposite: *Strikers at the factory gates of the Putilov metal works in St Petersburg, 1905*

51

warming themselves before bonfires at key points around the snowy square.

When Father Gapon's marchers reached the Narva Triumphal Arch they found the way blocked. Troops ordered them to turn back, but the marchers continued. The troops fired the usual three blank warning volleys, then live shots. Other workers approaching the square from different working-class areas were met by troops too. Within minutes their orderly ranks had broken in panic, and the snowy ground was scattered with bloodstained clothing, bodies and broken icons. The official figures said 96 people had been killed and 333 wounded. Many of these died later. Hundreds more injured marchers were probably carried away by friends and relatives and died at home. Some time afterwards, journalists presented to the Minister a list of 4,600 names of dead and wounded.

Nicholas's reaction to Bloody Sunday was, 'God, how sad and grim'. He wrote in his diary, 'A grim day. As a result of the desire of the workers to go to the Winter Palace, serious disorders took place in St Petersburg. In many parts of the city troops were compelled to fire. Many were killed or wounded.'

Father Gapon, a 'wanted' man, cut his hair and beard, gave up his priest's clothing, and fled to Switzerland. He still urged his followers to continue their struggle for freedom, but he was distrusted by some revolutionaries who thought he was a police spy who had deliberately set a trap to cause trouble between the workers and the government. In the spring of 1906 a revolutionary discovered him hiding in a little cottage in Finland, and murdered him.

Opposite: *Father Gapon, the Russian priest and leader of the workers*

7 Mutiny and Revolution, 1905

'Chuck the stinking stuff overboard.'

'We won't eat it. Even the Japs wouldn't feed us with stuff like this.' In 1905 there was trouble on board the Potemkin, Russia's largest new battleship in the Black Sea fleet. The men had seen their meat, slung on hooks on deck in the hot June sunshine, crawling with juicy, wriggling, white maggots.

Captain Golikov, a heavily built, easy-going man, with carefully trimmed beard and large moustache, assembled his rebellious crew, while the ship's surgeon peered through his spectacles and pronounced the meat 'excellent'. True there were a few eggs, but they could be easily washed away with vinegar and water. An end to this nonsense.

'I shall send some of this meat in a bottle to be *analysed*, and report to the commander in chief. He will decide what will be done with you,' said Captain Golikov weakly. But the first officer was made of sterner stuff. He ordered a guard to bring out a sailcloth. They began to seize a few men at random. Some of the older sailors remembered how trouble-makers were tied together under a *tarpaulin* and shot.

Suddenly *mutiny* broke out. A short, energetic sailor called Matushenko, a revolutionary, yelled out, 'Don't shoot your own comrades. You can't shoot your own shipmates.'

Other shouts followed. 'Collect rifles and ammunition. We're taking over the ship.'

Furious, revengeful sailors swept below to collect weapons, neatly stacked ready for the summer exercises. Poor Captain Golikov was dragged on deck in shirt and underpants, minus his uniform. He and the officers were shot, and thrown overboard. Crumpled sailcloth, bloodstained caps, and huddled bodies of men killed in the fighting covered the deck.

Matushenko soon hoisted the red revolutionary flag, and took command. He told the men to wash down the decks, and work normally. They had plenty of food and drink, and powerful guns. Other Black Sea battleships would soon follow the Potemkin's courageous lead. All Russia was merely waiting to overthrow the Tsar and slavery. They would soon be joined by workers in Odessa. The sailors obeyed, many with sinking hearts: they all knew the punishment for mutiny was death.

Odessa, a flourishing port of half a million people, was Russia's fourth largest city. It had splendid shops and a fine cathedral and university. The harbour was always full of ships laden with fish and *caviare*, timber and maize. But there was great poverty too. Down by the docks were wooden shacks, dingy factories and wretched hostels. Since the spring there had been serious strikes, bombs thrown in the city centre, and huge demonstrations of dockers, ironworkers and revolutionary students.

The Potemkin crew landed to buy provisions, and to bury with honour the first sailor killed in the mutiny. On his jumper they pinned a notice for their Odessa comrades to read: 'Here lies the body of Gregori Vakulinchuk, a sailor savagely killed by the senior officer of the battleship Potemkin for complaining that the soup was bad. Hurrah for freedom.' Weeping women, sympathetic workers and strikers joined them at the quayside.

Between Odessa's city centre and the harbour lies a sloping garden with an impressive granite staircase of 240 steps. These are the famous Richelieu steps, twelve great sweeping flights, each separated by wide platforms. Hundreds of people had collected on the steps and on the quay below. Suddenly regiments of galloping Cossacks arrived. In their crisp white jackets, black breeches and high black boots, they bore down relentlessly on horseback with whips, rifles and raised *sabres*. There was a flurry of sticks, a cascade of stones, the glint of 55 metal. The Cossacks knelt at the top of the staircase and fired at the teeming mass below, advanced twelve steps to the next broad platform and fired again. The panic-stricken crowd screamed, struggled, pushed in every direction to get free. A few minutes later all was silent on the splendid Richelieu steps, scattered with bits of bloodstained clothing and bodies.

For the next two days there was terrifying disorder in Odessa. Looters raided warehouses and carried off bags of sugar, grain and cotton. Unruly gangs set fire to shops and factories. By the time police and soldiers had restored order, thousands of people had perished, and a quarter of the city lay in smoking ruins.

The Potemkin crew played no part in all this. Matushenko ordered a *bombardment* of government buildings to help the workers, but as his men did not know which they were, or understand how the ship's new guns worked, they did little damage.

Meanwhile the Tsar had demanded the removal of 'this shameful blot on the honour of his fighting forces'. The admiral at Sebastopol sent five great battleships to attack the Potemkin, but on these ships too the crews were unreliable. One sailor noticed 'the officers were terribly uneasy, walking about in a dispirited manner and whispering together'. The admiral soon ordered the ships back to Sebastopol where the men were sent ashore on long leave. He admitted weakly, 'I am afraid the sea is controlled by rebels, and I have decided not to come out for the present.'

Only one ship, the George, decided to join the Potemkin. But having sent the officers ashore in small boats, her untrained crew failed to notice a mud bank in Odessa harbour, and were soon aground. They were all seized, imprisoned, or shot as mutineers.

The despairing Potemkin crew realised they could not carry out revolution singlehanded. Their mutiny now was world news. All shipping in the Black Sea was on the look-out for the rebel vessel and she was running short of coal. Matushenko hunted frantically through the captain's library books to find out their legal position. He was discouraged to discover that deserters could be *extradited* from friendly ports, and returned to their own country for punishment. Broken-hearted, he threw the red flag overboard.

Then the mutineers received a friendly message from King Carol I of Romania. If they surrendered, they would not be harmed. Matushenko opened the *sea cocks* and sank the Potemkin before he and his comrades rowed ashore. The crew became Romanian citizens; some found work in the docks and factories, and some married Romanian girls. A few emigrated to Argentina with money collected from English well-wishers. In 1907 Nicholas offered an *amnesty* to Russian offenders.

Matushenko returned to Russia, to see his family, or even perhaps to start another revolution. He was seized at the frontier and hanged as a traitor. Ten years later the successful revolution of which he had dreamed came about. And, in the famous Russian film about the battleship Potemkin, Matushenko and the mutinous crew were shown as heroes.

YEAR OF REVOLUTION – 1905

Bloody Sunday marked the beginning of a terrible year of revolution throughout the Russian empire. In big cities like Warsaw, St Petersburg, Moscow, Kiev and Riga, thousands of workers went on strike. In January alone 500,000 men were idle, more than the combined number of strikers in the ten years before: gasworks, electric power stations, oil wells, docks, railways and factories were all affected. The industrial workers were beginning to realise their power.

Meanwhile leaders of the non-Russian nationalities (Baltic peoples, Finns, Poles, Ukrainians and Jews) were demanding equal rights and respect for their customs and languages. Ten thousand troops had to be sent to Georgia in the Caucasus to restore order that autumn. In the Black Sea fleet there was the most serious naval mutiny in Russia's history, while railwaymen on the T.S.R, organised by Bolshevik revolutionaries, refused to run trains to Manchuria. They demanded a parlia- 57

ment, higher wages and an end to the war. Even the peasants became violent. Nearly a million had suffered as soldiers in the Japanese war. Others, part time workers in the towns, were stirred up by revolutionaries. Desperate after bad harvests, many murdered their landlords, burned manor houses, and cut down valuable timber. Only the Cossack troops could be completely relied upon; they were still loyal to the Tsar and contemptuous of the masses.

In February Nicholas was shocked to hear that a socialist revolutionary had killed the Grand Duke Sergei, married to Alexandra's sister, with a bomb, in Moscow. It was the first *assassination* of a member of the royal family since Nicholas's grandfather was murdered in 1881.

Revolutionaries were busy everywhere organising workers' committees (*soviets*). They smuggled in weapons from abroad, trained groups in street fighting, and handed secretly printed revolutionary pamphlets to soldiers. The *liberals*, men who wanted Russia to have some form of parliamentary government, were active too. Most of them were businessmen, doctors, lawyers, journalists and zemstvo members (county councillors) who wanted to secure reform by peaceful means, but agreed with the revolutionaries on many points. They attended dinners and meetings to discuss improvements, and petitioned the Tsar.

Their demands tell us a lot about what Russia was like under Nicholas II. They asked for a parliament, elected by everyone by a secret vote. This assembly, or *Duma*, should pass laws and control money matters. The Duma, not the Tsar, should choose ministers. All peoples in the Empire should be treated equally, whatever their nationality. There should be freedom of speech and writing, and the right to travel, to form trade unions, and to practise different religions. There should be fairer taxation, free primary education, pensions, and better working conditions. More land should be taken from the Tsar, the church and the nobles and given to the peasants, whose redemption taxes should be ended.

Moderate people hoped to change Russia gradually through acts of parliament. The revolutionaries wanted to overthrow the Tsar and set up a republic. They wanted banks, land, railways and factories to be given to the people. The Social Democrats, who included the Bolsheviks, supported strikes and aimed to seize power by an armed uprising. The Socialist Revolutionaries favoured assassinations and terror.

WHAT NICHOLAS DID

As discontent grew, Nicholas's ministers took stronger measures. His ruthless chief of police forbade demonstrations, brought in more troops and police, and moved into a wing of the Winter Palace. However in February the Tsar granted some reforms. He gave his subjects the right to petition him. Earlier he had regarded Russian hopes of a parliament as 'senseless dreams', but now he promised to summon a parliament or Duma.

But these promises only led to more strikes, disorder and further demands for reform. Nicholas wrote to his mother, 'It makes me sick to read the news. Nothing but new strikes in schools and factories, murdered policemen, Cossacks, soldiers, riots, disorders and mutinies.' His ministers, he complained, only fluttered about like a lot of frightened hens instead of making firm decisions. His mother sensibly urged him to reappoint Witte as chief minister: 'He is a man of genius, energetic and clearsighted.'

Witte was by far the ablest of Nicholas's ministers and had done a lot to modernise Russia. He developed industries, encouraged the building of the T.S.R. and made useful trading treaties with other countries. Witte advised the Tsar that to let things drift would lead to chaos. Russia was ready for a different kind of government. Nicholas's only hope was to allow the people greater freedom immediately. He must summon a parliament and not interfere with its decisions.

In October Nicholas agreed, his heart 'filled with a great and painful grief'. He ended the redemption payments made by peasants. On paper, promises were made of better conditions for Jews, Poles and other nationalities. He summoned a Duma in 1906, but only the wealthiest people in the Empire were allowed to vote in elections, so it did not really represent the country. Four Dumas met before the revolution of 1917, and each was given less and less power.

Count Sergei Witte, minister of the Tsar

The Tsar still appointed his ministers, and controlled the army, navy, judges and foreign affairs. Trotsky said, 'Everything is given and nothing is given.' Meetings could be held, but they were surrounded by troops. Free speech was granted, but *censorship* existed as before. The universities were occupied by troops, the prisons overflowing. In 1906 and 1907 there were frightful massacres of Jews, and the army killed thousands of peasants.

Cavalry troops keeping order in the Moscow streets during the year of revolution, 1905. Notice people travelling by sledge in the snowy weather

The 1905 revolution did not really teach Nicholas anything. He did not seize his chance to make real reforms to save his throne. Uneasy peace had been restored – for a time. Blindly Nicholas continued to rule in the old way. The Bolsheviks learned much more. Lenin called the 1905 revolution a 'dress rehearsal'. The revolutionaries discovered how much havoc workers could cause if their strikes and demonstrations were properly planned by well organised leaders. They realised, too, that revolution would not succeed until the Tsar's soldiers also joined the workers.

8 Rasputin

Gregori Rasputin came from a remote Siberian village, 320 kilometres east of the Ural mountains, and eight days by rail, steamer and cart from St Petersburg (see the map on page 5). This was steppe land where grass could grow as high as a man. The lush meadows were dotted with silver birch groves, low hills, lakes and bogs; forget-me-nots, irises and primroses carpeted the forest clearings in spring; in summer tiny wild strawberries were everywhere. Peasants wearing long belted rough shirts and baggy trousers, and girls, in gay cotton dresses and bright scarves, cut hay and harvested grain in the scorching sunshine.

The people of Siberia were bold, rough and independent. Some were descended from banished convicts. Others were sturdy peasants who had travelled east from their overcrowded villages. Gregori's father was headman of the village and owned twelve cows and eighteen strong Siberian horses. The family suffered like all peasants. Their cottage was destroyed by fire, and hail sometimes ruined the harvest. Gregori's mother died young, and two of his brothers were drowned in the swift-flowing river Tura.

Gregori's father was religious, between his drunken lapses. He read the Bible every night to his family. Gregori learnt little at school, being a lazy boy, but he had a good memory and always remembered the Bible passages. He became a daring coachman, travelling long distances by sledge in winter on glistening snow-covered roads through forests of Siberian cedars and firs. He married a local peasant girl, but he was a lonely, restless fellow who spent years away from home, wandering thousands of kilometres on foot as a pilgrim to distant holy cities. People were used in Russia to meeting holy men in ragged dress with long, *unkempt* hair and beards.

During his travels Rasputin visited Kiev, a fairytale city of golden domes and silver bell towers, and pink houses with green roofs. Here, on the wooded banks of the river Dnieper, Russian Christianity had its earliest centre. He saw the magnificent Santa Sophia cathedral with its rich pictures, *mosaics* and fifteen gilded domes spangled with stars; in the tombs below were bones of a hundred saints. He went to Kazan, too, an old Tartar city, with splendid *mosques*. Here was the miracle-working icon of the Virgin of Kazan. He wandered still further afield to beautiful monasteries perched on rocky crags at Mount Athos in Greece. He also travelled to Damascus, and Bethlehem, Nazareth and Jerusalem.

In 1905 Rasputin went to St Petersburg. His simple, honest faith appealed to some clergy, including Bishop Hermogen. He soon had many admirers, too, among the nobility, especially ladies. They were attracted by this new character in their elegant world – a real peasant. They offered him wines, *caviare* and other delicacies at their fashionable parties, and listened spellbound to his wise words. Dressed in long black robes, with a huge cross on his chest, the holy man heard their confessions regularly, offered advice, and was said to have powers of healing. He lived very simply and seldom accepted money.

Many people, however, were revolted by Rasputin's peasant ways. 'His face was of the most ordinary peasant type, a coarse oval with large ugly features, overgrown with a *slovenly* beard, and a very long nose.' His table manners were disgusting, and he smelt like a goat. There were stories of drunken parties at his house, and of an energetic Rasputin enjoying himself with the wild gypsy people who lived on the outskirts of the capital. Then he wore peasant boots, and stuffed a coarse peasant blouse into wide trousers, drank himself into a *stupor*, and danced with gypsy girls to frenzied music till early morning. He told his reproachful admirers later, 'There is no holy man on earth. So long as man lives, he sins.' Rasputin believed everyone had to sin, and repent, regularly to be saved.

Gregori Rasputin, who was murdered in December 1916

Rasputin met the royal family through Anna Vyroubova, the Tsarina's lady-in-waiting, one of his most devoted admirers. In November 1905, Nicholas wrote in his diary, 'We have got to know a man of God, Gregori, from the Tobolsk province'. Rasputin gained influence over Alexandra because it seemed he could relieve Alexei's haemophilia when the usual doctors failed. The frantic Tsarina, frightened that her darling son would die, was calmed by Rasputin's soothing words, and ready to trust 'Our Friend' completely.

Rasputin certainly had strange healing powers and *hypnotic* influence. Enemies and friends alike noticed his extraordinary eyes – 'His keen and penetrating gaze did in fact convey a feeling of some hidden supernatural force.' The 'holy man' 65 treated Alexei on several occasions, and the boy's grateful mother would hear nothing bad said about him.

Alexei's most severe illness occurred one autumn, in 1912. The royal family were shooting *bison* in Poland. The eight-year-old Tsarevich bruised his left thigh severely against a boat while rowing on the lake. Anna Vyroubova remembered his tremendous suffering: 'The next weeks were endless torment to the boy and all of us who had to listen to his constant cries. For fully eleven days those dreadful sounds filled the corridors outside his room.' For a fortnight Alexandra never undressed or went to bed, but sat for hours at the little boy's bedside. He lay huddled, half conscious, on his side, with his leg drawn up under his chin. It was nearly a year before he could straighten it properly afterwards. Three doctors said Alexei's case was hopeless, and in desperation Alexandra telegraphed Rasputin in Siberia to pray for him. Rasputin replied by telegraph, 'Do not grieve. The little one will not die.' A day later the bleeding stopped.

Rasputin became more and more unpopular, and there were several unsuccessful attempts on his life. His enemies included Nicholas's more sensible ministers, like Stolypin, who managed to get him sent away from court for a while. Leading clergy now regarded him as a fraud, not a 'holy man'. When war broke out in 1914 Rasputin's influence over the royal family, through the Tsarina, became even more harmful. He, and the Tsarina, were accused by their enemies of being German spies. In 1915 Nicholas went to lead his troops at the front, leaving Alexandra and Rasputin in control of the Government at St Petersburg. Alexandra always listened to his advice, rather than to that of more able men, and unsuitable friends of Rasputin's were appointed as ministers.

The third time Rasputin saved the Tsarevich's life was in 1915. He announced prophetically, 'It is the last time I shall be able to save him.'

THE END OF RASPUTIN

66   In 1916 a group of Rasputin's enemies decided that to murder

him was the only way to save Russia from his evil influence. The plotters were a doctor, a member of the Duma called Purishkevich, and Grand Duke Dmitri, cousin of the Tsar. Their leader was Prince Felix Yusopov, a handsome, elegant young nobleman who had been educated at Oxford, and at the most select officers' military college in Russia. His family was enormously rich and owned three palaces in St Petersburg, and others in Moscow and the Crimea. Yusopov had married the Tsar's niece Irina. He later wrote a book describing how the murder was planned and carried out.

Rasputin was tremendously flattered when Yusopov invited him to attend a special party very late one night, and promised to collect him by car. He put on a clean white silk blouse embroidered with cornflowers, trousers of black velvet, and long new boots. Yusopov remembered that his face smelt of fresh, cheap soap. He had carefully combed his hair and beard.

The room in Yusopov's splendid house was warm, welcoming, and dimly lit. A cheerful log fire burned in the hearth and a large white bearskin rug covered the polished granite floor. Scattered about were beautiful little tables laden with delicious cakes and dainties. They had been sliced open and filled with poison – powdered potassium cyanide crystals. The wine was strongly poisoned too.

In the background a gramophone softly played the latest hit tunes, but there was no sign of other guests. Nervously Yusopov took up his guitar and played some of Rasputin's favourite folksongs. The superhuman Rasputin ate the cakes, and drank several glasses of poisoned wine, with no apparent ill effects. Finally, in desperation, about two o'clock, Yusopov went upstairs, seized a revolver and shot him. There was a roar like a wild beast. Rasputin fell heavily on the bearskin rug. 'The bullet had passed through the region of the heart. There could be no doubt about it. He was dead.'

But Rasputin started dragging himself out of the room and across the snow-covered courtyard. Purishkevich, another of the assassins, had to fire four more shots before the body slumped into a pile of snow. Then they wrapped it in an old 67

blue curtain, tied it with rope, and drove off quickly by car. In their haste and excitement, they forgot to attach the weights they had brought before they threw the body over a bridge into the river Neva, nor did they notice that they had dropped one of Rasputin's boots in the snow.

A policeman arrived at Yusopov's house. He enquired about the shots and bloodstains in the snow. Yusopov explained: one of his drunken friends at a party had accidentally shot an old dog in the yard. He remarked coolly, 'My wife is a niece of the Tsar. Members of the imperial family and their houses are *inviolable*. Measures cannot be taken against them, except by order of his majesty the Emperor himself.'

Many people knew who had murdered Rasputin. Nicholas said, 'I am filled with shame that the hands of my kinsmen are stained with the blood of a peasant.' However he did not bring the offenders to trial, or punish them severely. Yusopov was merely sent in disgrace to his country estate (after the revolution he lived abroad). Grand Duke Dmitri was ordered to serve with the Russian army in Persia and the others went free.

A few days after the murder, Rasputin's boot lying in the snow provided the clue to his whereabouts. The ice was broken, and his frozen body recovered from the river, but only the grief-stricken Tsarina and his few friends at court mourned Rasputin's death. They buried him quietly at Tsarskoe Selo but he was still not at peace. A few months later, when revolution broke out, rough soldiers broke into the church, dug up his body, carried it to the nearby forest, and burnt it.

The day before he was murdered Rasputin had written a letter to the Tsar – to be opened only when he died. In it he expressed a strange *foreboding* that he would die before the new year. It contained a *prophetic* message to Nicholas. 'If it is one of your relatives who have brought about my death, then not one of your family will remain alive for more than two years.'

Opposite: *The splendid palace of Prince Yusopov in St Petersburg where Rasputin was killed*

9 *War and Revolution, 1917*

Revolution came one stage nearer when Russia became involved in the First World War in the summer of 1914. The causes of war were complicated and the details need not concern us here. For some time the great European powers had been involved in colonial disputes. They had also enlarged their armies and navies and developed rival alliances. Germany, Austria-Hungary and Italy formed the Triple Alliance, while Russia was linked with England and France in a looser Triple Entente. Conflict broke out between the two groups.

On the outbreak of war a great patriotic outburst of loyalty to the Tsar swept through Russia. The German-sounding St Petersburg was renamed Petrograd, and Nicholas, in simple khaki uniform, appeared before wildly cheering crowds. In the marble hall of the Winter Palace he took a solemn oath: 'I solemnly swear that I will never make peace as long as a single enemy remains on Russian soil.'

While England and France fought against Germany on the Western Front in northern France and Belgium, Russia fought mainly on the Eastern Front. This great area of Russian Poland, 320 kilometres long, separated Russia from her enemies, Germany and Austria-Hungary. It was a thinly defended stretch of vast forest and marshland with few roads. Russia might attack Germany from the Polish capital, Warsaw, a fortress city on the river Vistula (see map on page 5).

However, Russia had only six railway lines from Warsaw to the front and few branch lines enabling her to shift men quickly from north to south. Germany had seventeen railway lines leading to the battle areas and Austria had seven. They could concentrate vast forces speedily. Russia had the largest army among the great powers and could muster huge extra reserves of peasants, but she was badly equipped, with few modern weapons. To increase the war effort, Nicholas banned the sale of vodka to all factory workers.

In August 1914 France encouraged her Russian ally to launch an attack against Germany, as this would divert German attention from the Western Front. So the commander-in-chief, Grand Duke Nicholas, the Tsar's uncle, an enormously tall and energetic man, ordered troops to attack the East Prussian area of Germany. The German generals, Hindenburg and Ludendorf, defeated his armies overwhelmingly at the battle of Tannenberg. A month later the Russians were again badly beaten, and expelled from East Prussia. They were more successful against the Austrian armies in Galicia, but Hindenburg discovered the secret code of Russian radio messages, and knew their troop movements. He rushed troops from East Prussia to help his Austrian allies.

By 1915 Russia had lost more than two million men, half of them taken prisoner. Clothing and ammunition were in short supply through corruption and mismanagement. At home, there was little food in the large cities, and people were weary of war. In the autumn Alexandra persuaded Nicholas to take personal command of the army, and send the Grand Duke Nicholas to an unimportant battle area. This was a mistake as it meant that the Tsar himself could be blamed for military failures. It also left Alexandra and the unpopular Rasputin in control of the government: both were accused of being German spies. This was unfair to Alexandra whose letters to the Tsar show how much she hated the Germans.

Alexandra turned the large palace at Tsarskoe Selo into a military hospital. She took a course in first-aid with her elder daughters, and spent many hours visiting sick and wounded soldiers. She wrote encouraging letters to Nicholas at the front almost daily. 'Never have they seen such firmness in you before. You are proving yourself the autocrat without which Russia cannot exist. Being firm is our only saving. I know what it costs you.'

Alexandra now received regular reports from ministers, but the real power was Rasputin's. The aged prime minister, Goremykin, was replaced by a series of ministers whom Rasputin suggested. They came and went with bewildering speed, and made long-term planning impossible.

Nicholas took Alexei with him to his army headquarters at Mogilev in Poland. They lived simply in the governor's house, and slept on hard camp beds. To raise *morale*, the troops paraded regularly past their Tsar. Gilliard, Alexei's tutor, remembered how proudly and defiantly they held their heads up, despite their crippling defeats. He was greatly impressed, too, that 'the eleven-year-old Tsarevich wore the uniform of a private, with nothing to distinguish it from that of any boy in the service'.

In December Alexei developed a heavy cold, and his sneezing brought on a severe nosebleed. He made a terribly painful journey back to Tsarskoe Selo. Again the Tsarina felt grateful to 'Our Friend', Rasputin, who, she was convinced, had stopped the bleeding.

During the summer of 1916 the Russians launched their last major attack. General Brusilov, who had successfully studied German military tactics, thrust deep into Austria, at first with great success. Then the Germans, with their superior railways, shifted troops rapidly from the north and halted them. Brusilov had forced the Germans to remove troops from the west, and so had helped France. He had encouraged the Romanians to enter the war on the allied side, and he had greatly weakened Austria. All this would ultimately contribute to Germany's defeat, but it had been achieved with tremendous casualties.

Russians faced a terrible winter in 1916–17. It was bitterly cold with the temperature falling to forty degrees below zero. Essential railways were almost at a standstill. In Petrograd the cost of living had risen three times more than wages, and it was impossible to obtain much vital food. Women and children wasted hours outside empty shops, queuing in vain for rationed bread. They returned home to their cold, damp hovels, unwarmed through shortage of coal and firewood. Many families had lost a father, son or brother at the front. The working classes were becoming increasingly hostile to the government, and took part in illegal strikes. Revolutionaries were busy in factories and at street corners, distributing weapons and illegal leaflets. As they won support from disheartened soldiers deserting from the front, the situation became more dangerous.

The police, always on the alert, reported that serious riots involving hundreds of casualties were likely to break out. Nicholas seemed unaware of the dangerous situation, although his mother sent him warning letters. The British ambassador, Sir George Buchanan, also took the trouble to visit his headquarters and tell him of the serious disorders in the capital. Rasputin's murder in December left the Empress grief-stricken.

Then the Emperor began to lose heart. 'Nicholas II now feels himself overwhelmed and dominated by events. He has *abdicated* inwardly and is now resigned to disaster', wrote the French ambassador in his diary. Nicholas asked the president of the Duma about this time, 'Is it possible that for twenty-two years I have tried to act for the best, and for twenty-two years it was all a mistake?'

REVOLUTIONS

The situation changed rapidly in Russia in 1917. Two revolutions took place. You can read the detailed story in 'Lenin and the Russian Revolution', another Then and There book. In February (March by the Western calendar) angry crowds paraded through the streets of Petrograd, carrying red flags and shouting, 'Down with the German woman' (the Tsarina). Bakeries and foodshops were looted, but the troops, earlier so loyal to the Tsar, refused to shoot the hungry people. Ministers telephoned the Tsar, begging him to return from the front, but Nicholas's reply was to forbid the Duma to meet. The Duma decided to defy him and take power itself. Its

Kerensky, Prime Minister of the provisional government which was overthrown by the Bolsheviks in the autumn of 1917

members elected a *provisional* government with Prince Lvov as Prime Minister, and Kerensky, a young lawyer, as Minister of Justice (he was shortly to replace Lvov as Prime Minister). Meanwhile the upper classes enjoyed their gay life in the smart restaurants and theatres. Ballets were still performed. Plays and concerts continued. Alexandra was busy at Tsarskoe Selo nursing her family who had caught measles.

At the army headquarters Nicholas met his generals. Duke Nicholas and Generals Brusilov and Russki strongly urged the Tsar to give up the throne to avoid *civil war*. He was preparing to do so when members of the Duma arrived to insist on his abdication. Nicholas received them, kindly and quietly, in his imperial railway carriage lined with green silk. They sensed that the dignified, withdrawn man, with tired eyes sunken in hollow cheekbones, was almost relieved to give up power at last. To Nicholas 'all around was treachery, cowardice and defeat'. He suggested that his brother Michael should succeed him, as Alexei was not strong enough to become Tsar, but Michael wisely refused. Nicholas was allowed to return to Tsarskoe Selo where the royal family were placed under house arrest, largely for their own safety. A little later Kerensky moved them to Tobolsk in Siberia.

The members of the new provisional government were honest and well-meaning, but they had little experience of ruling and were out of touch with the people. While they were busy trying to help their allies to continue the war, and discussing the new type of rule Russia should have, the workers of Petrograd were seizing power. Their active committee (soviet) met in another part of the same Tauride palace where the official government was meeting. Soldiers, peasants and workers wanted reforms quickly – an end to the war, land taken from the landlords and given to the peasants, food and better conditions for the townspeople. Lenin, Trotsky and other Bolshevik leaders returned from exile abroad to rouse the people with stirring speeches and to organise them. As one Bolshevik worker said, 'All the comrades groped about in darkness till the arrival of Lenin.' But it was several months before Lenin was actually in a position to lead a revolution.

However, by October (November in the western calendar) Bolsheviks had control of important factories, post offices, power stations and railway stations. The provisional government was overthrown. Kerensky and other ministers fled into exile. All those who had worked for a parliament, liberal reforms and individual freedom in Russia were bitterly disappointed.

The Bolsheviks signed a humiliating peace with Germany, at Brestlitovsk in Poland in 1918. Russia handed over her

Baltic provinces, and the fertile Ukraine, the 'bread basket' of Russia. If Germany had not been defeated shortly afterwards and returned her gains, Russia would have lost a third of her people and her agriculture, and more than half her industry.

Fortunately Nicholas did not live to see Lenin, and later Stalin, ruling as ruthlessly as any Tsar, controlling the press more rigidly than in his own time, using a secret police harsher and more *sinister* than his had been. More people were sent to labour camps in Siberia than he had ever punished. The Bolsheviks persecuted the Orthodox Church he and his family loved. Noble families were driven into exile to London, Paris and New York. The peasants, after much bloodshed, farmed the land, not individually as many of them had hoped, but carefully controlled, under state supervision. The glittering splendour of St Petersburg with its music, ballet and close links with the West was a thing of the past. For many years Russia became isolated, concentrating on its own affairs.

Yet many millions of poor Russians, workers and peasants, regarded the revolution as a blessing. Their lives were much better than they had been under the Tsars. For good or ill the old Russia had disappeared for ever. A new state, the modern U.S.S.R, was born.

10 Murder at Ekaterinburg?

A NEW PRISON

In April 1918 the Bolsheviks decided to move the royal family from Tobolsk to Ekaterinburg, an important mining town in the Ural mountains. Nicholas said he would rather have gone anywhere than the Urals where the workers were bitterly hostile to him.

In Ekaterinburg the Bolsheviks seized a large brick house belonging to a rich merchant called Ipatiev. Local people called it 'the House of Special Purpose'. The royal family, with Dr Botkin, a cook, a maid and a manservant, were crowded into six upper rooms. Their windows were painted white, so they could not see out. The Bolsheviks built two strong wooden fences round the house, and put a machine-gun in the attic. Fifty guards patrolled the small garden plot from sentry boxes, and other guards inside had revolvers.

Conditions were harsh indeed that summer. The guards, drunken, untidy men from local factories and mines, spied on the royal family continuously. They ate with 'citizen Romanov' and seized the food first. They interrupted conversation with loud laughter and rude stories. Sometimes they stole the girls' things.

One more sympathetic guard remembered Nicholas on his fiftieth birthday. He got the impression Nicholas was a simple, kindly, talkative person. His hair was greying, his gentle eyes tired and sunken, he wore an old khaki soldier's uniform, and worn out boots. The Tsarina, who also had her birthday that May, was forty-six but appeared older. The guards decided she looked exactly like a Tsarina – grave and haughty.

The house of Ipatiev where the royal family were imprisoned in Ekaterinburg

Every morning the royal family got up at eight for morning prayers. They had tea and stale black bread for breakfast, and for lunch thin, watery soup and meat rissoles brought in from the local soviet canteen and warmed up by their cook. The table was bare, without linen or silverware. Each day was the same, spent in reading, knitting, singing hymns to drown the soldiers' revolutionary songs below, and short walks in the garden plot under strict guard. Alexei was very weak, and usually in bed. The Tsarina, with her bad heart, often rested too. The only links with the outside world were the priest who occasionally came to take services, and local nuns who brought milk and eggs for the Tsarevich.

Nevertheless, the royal family seemed serene, dignified and completely united. Perhaps were buoyed up by hopes of release. Gibbes and Gilliard, the royal tutors, were in Ekaterinburg, frantically trying, through the British Consul, to organise their rescue. It was madness, with 10,000 Red soldiers (the revolutionaries) in the town, and spies at every corner. Then

came rumours of large White armies (Tsarist supporters) helped by the allies, moving against the Reds. Would they save the royal family? Or would their advance make the communists panic, and encourage them to get rid of their prisoners quickly?

Most people think that the Romanovs were murdered in July 1918, a few days before Ekaterinburg fell to the Whites, and the Reds retreated to Perm 320 kilometres away; yet their bodies were never discovered. Here is the usual story.

In July the drunken, thieving guards were replaced by Letts from the Baltic provinces, Magyars (Hungarian prisoners of war) and others who would ask no questions. Their leader was Jacob Yurovsky, a Russian watchmaker and photographer closely in touch with the Cheka, the Bolshevik secret police which was set up in 1918. About midnight on 16 July he told the royal family and servants to dress quickly as the Whites were approaching, and they were to be moved. The group collected in the basement room downstairs. The Tsar, Alexandra and Alexei were given chairs, while the others stood near the wall with the girls' little spaniel, Jemmy. Suddenly Yurovsky called out, 'Your relatives have tried to save you and have failed. We must now shoot you.'

He and his guards shot them all brutally with revolvers. Anastasia, who had only fainted, regained consciousness and screamed. She was hit on the head with a rifle butt and stabbed to death. Then the guards removed the women's jewellery, gave it to Yurovsky, and bundled the bodies into a truck. They took the corpses about twenty-one kilometres outside the town to a gloomy wood with a mineshaft. It was called the Four Brothers, after four isolated pine trees nearby. There the bodies were hacked to pieces, covered with petrol and sulphuric acid, and burnt for three days. Any remains were thrown down the mineshaft. Yurovsky had meanwhile summoned the guards at Ipatiev house and told them to wash the blood off the floors.

Opposite: *Revolutionary soldiers guard their prisoner, the former Tsar Nicholas II, after his abdication. Compare this picture with the one on page 7*

About a week later Nicholas's supporters, the Whites, arrived in Ekaterinburg.

THE WHITES INVESTIGATE

How do we know this is what really happened? If you read detective stories you will know that successful solving of the murder depends on having a keen, *impartial* detective who goes quickly to the scene of the crime. He is not led astray by interfering people or false clues. He interviews reliable people, and examines the body carefully. Now see what happened at Ekaterinburg.

On capturing Ekaterinburg the Whites started an enquiry. They employed several investigators who did not agree, and were constantly being upset by army officers. They could not find anyone who had actually seen the shooting. (Yurovsky and other key guards had probably been captured and shot while fighting the Whites.) The Tsar's mother, living in southern Russia, and George V, Nicholas's English cousin, sent other people to find out what was happening. Newspaper correspondents, foreign spies, and the British Consul in Siberia all listened to rumours, and drew their own conclusions. All this time civil war was raging in the area, and within a few months the Whites had to retreat, and abandon their enquiry.

Nicholai Sokolov, the chief White 'detective', was a keen Tsarist supporter. He was a small, intense man, with an irritating habit of twitching his moustache, and a nervous manner, partly caused by a glass eye. He had studied law in the Ukraine and was a 'Court Investigator for Specially Important Cases'. When the Reds recaptured Ekaterinburg, he fled across Siberia and eventually reached Paris, with his valuable files of notes. In 1924 he wrote a book in French called '*Judicial* Enquiry into the assassination of the Russian Royal Family'. A little later a Russian version appeared. Everyone accepted Sokolov's story as the official account of what had happened, but he died of a heart attack in 1924 before he could really enjoy his triumph.

Sokolov collected masses of information at Ekaterinburg. With his helpers, he examined the basement room at Ipatiev house carefully, removed bullets, and took measurements and photographs. He listed all the belongings of the royal family, left behind by the Reds – dirty linen, books, cold cream, medicine bottles, notepaper and pieces of girls' hair. Sokolov also interviewed soldiers and others. Peasants described how, while travelling by cart to sell fish in Ekaterinburg, they had passed near the wood by the 'Four Brothers'. Red soldiers with guns roughly turned them away, 'Don't look back, or we'll shoot.'

Of course, being curious, the peasants returned later, and found the remains of bonfires, burnt clothing and broken jewels (the princesses had sewn their jewels into their underclothes for safekeeping). 'Merciful Christ, can they have burnt the whole family alive?' asked one peasant.

Sokolov later made a detailed list, and photographed the objects found in the wood and at the mineshaft. There were charred bones, remains of a finger, parts of clothing worn by the Tsar and Alexei, and many earrings, pearls, bracelets, shoe buckles and metal corset ribs. Gilliard and Gibbes later identified the jewellery as belonging to the royal family. Heaps of 'clues' had been found.

THE MYSTERY REMAINS

Not everyone completely agrees with Sokolov's story. When producing a TV programme in 1971, two BBC writers, Tom Mangold and Anthony Summers, started a new investigation. They spent four years interviewing old people all over the world who knew the last Romanovs. They studied the evidence afresh, and wrote a book called 'The File on the Tsar'.

First they had to find the seven huge files of original notes on which Sokolov had based his book. They had been kept by a British journalist and sold in London. They were finally tracked down in the library at Harvard University in America. Old wooden boxes, marked 'N. Sokolov', discovered in a Paris antique dealer's shop, contained his photographs of exhibits. There was also a mysterious black cloth bag which a foreigner had handed to a startled librarian at Stanford University, California, in 1936, with strict instructions not to open it for many years. It was untied after 1960, and found to contain more interesting Russian papers.

When Mangold and Summers studied the material afresh, they found that in his book Sokolov had left out evidence that went against his case. He had always believed that all the royal family had been killed by the Reds at Ipatiev house. Mangold and Summers thought that a lot of Sokolov's evidence seemed doubtful.

He had laid great stress on an important telegraph message seized by Whites at the Post Office when the Reds fled. It was written in a secret code of numbers (which Sokolov had decoded) by the local communist leader. It told the Moscow Bolsheviks that the royal family had been killed. Mangold and Summers thought it might be a *fake*. The local communist's signature at the bottom was quite unlike his handwriting on other documents.

Then there was a key witness, a Red guard who said he saw the bodies of the royal family minutes after the execution. He died very suddenly (they said of *typhus*) after giving his story to the Whites. Did he die a natural death or was he 'done away with' before he could change his story?

Mangold and Summers showed photographs of the finds at the mineshaft to police experts at Scotland Yard. They now use more scientific methods than in 1917. The police thought that even if bodies had been burnt with petrol and sulphuric acid for three days they would not have disappeared with so little trace. Surprisingly, no teeth, the most difficult things to destroy, had been found. The photograph of the little dog's body, too, showed that it was well preserved, and still furry. It could not possibly have been in the mineshaft all that time and must have been 'planted' there later.

Opposite: *Grand Duchess Anastasia, the youngest daughter of the Tsar*

Either Whites, or Reds, of course, could have tampered with objects at the mineshaft. The Whites obviously wanted to prove that brutal Reds had murdered the Tsar and all his family. The Reds could have killed only the Tsar and his servants, and created conditions to make it look as though the rest had perished too. They might, perhaps, have spirited the German-born Empress and the girls away, intending to use them as *hostages* in their secret talks with Germany.

If the royal family were not killed in the way Sokolov believed, then what happened to them? Their fate remains a mystery. Possibly Nicholas and Alexei were executed on a military parade-ground outside Ekaterinburg. The Tsarina and girls may have been taken to Perm by fleeing Bolsheviks. Various people thought they glimpsed the women in Perm several months later. They were closely guarded, wore rough soldiers' clothing, and had their hair cut short.

Railway workers at Perm told strange stories, too, of how the Tsar's youngest daughter had tried to escape. She had been brutally beaten up by Red soldiers in the woods when they recaptured her. A doctor in Perm had been hastily summoned to treat an injured girl who was badly bruised. She told him she was the Emperor's daughter, Anastasia, but the communist guards would not allow him to have further talks with her. We lose trace of what happened to Alexandra and her daughters by the autumn of 1918. For a while Tsarist supporters still hoped that the family was alive, hidden secretly perhaps in a remote church or house. From time to time Olga or Alexei were 'seen' in other parts of Europe, but these characters were probably *impostors*.

The legend that Anastasia survived persists. 'Anastasia' reappeared in 1920. A desperate young Russian girl tried to commit suicide by jumping into a canal in Berlin, eighteen months after the royal family had vanished from Ekaterinburg. She had an injury to her head, and suffered from loss of memory and poor health. She spent many years in a dazed state in German and Swiss hospitals. Some distant members of the royal family who visited her were convinced she was an impostor. This frail, weak girl was so unlike the merry tomboy they had known. Others were amazed to find she could remember details of life at the Russian court. She also shared certain features with the real Anastasia – the little mole on her shoulder and the distorted joints on her big toes. Articles, books and films were produced about 'Anastasia', and endless court cases tried to prove, or disprove, that she was the youngest daughter of the Tsar. By the 1970s 'Anastasia' was a quiet, modest old lady called Anna Anderson, married to a retired American history professor, and living in Virginia. Perhaps she preferred to blot out from her mind the troubles of her 'other life'.

Communist accounts tell us even less about the end of the Romanovs than White accounts, or modern Western theories. The local soviet (workmen, peasants and Red guards) of the Urals reported on 21 July 1918 that because Ekaterinburg was being threatened by Whites they had shot ex-Tsar Nicholas Romanov as 'guilty before the people of innumerable bloody crimes'. The Bolsheviks in Moscow under Sverdlov announced their approval. Nothing was said about other members of the royal family.

Trotsky, who had proposed a public trial, once asked Sverdlov in Moscow who had decided to have Nicholas shot. Sverdlov replied, 'We decided it here. Ilych [Lenin] believed we shouldn't leave the Whites a live banner to rally round.'

In 1919 the communist newspaper 'Pravda' announced that twenty-eight people had been tried in Perm for murdering the royal family, and fourteen were found guilty and executed. The trial, including made up names of the 'guilty' people, may have been an attempt to improve relations with Western countries by making it appear that the murderers were being punished. The official communist account at present is that: 'In July 1918 the provincial committee at Ekaterinburg took a decision to execute Nicholas II and his family and *retinue* when the Whites started an *offensive*.'

Ekaterinburg is now renamed Sverdlovsk after one of the Bolshevik leaders. Ipatiev house, freshly painted regularly, 87 is the local communist party office. Children in Russian schools read communist history books which teach them that Lenin is the founder of their country's greatness. They spend little time learning about the last Tsar.

How Do We Know?

Hundreds of books have been written about Russia in the time of Nicholas II, and though many old records have disappeared fresh material appears every year. For example, when new sewage works were carried out in Odessa in 1927 under the old police station, many papers belonging to the Tsarist secret police were discovered. One of the problems of this period is that people still feel very strongly for and against the revolution. Their writings are *biased*. Soviet historians are obviously keen supporters of revolutionary leaders whereas some Western writers tend to be more sympathetic to the Tsar and his family, and admire what was good in 'old Russia'.

Here are some of the ways in which I found out more about Russia under the last Tsar. I read:

1. Private letters of Nicholas, his mother and Alexandra.
2. Karl Baedeker's *Russia*, a guide book published in 1914 for foreign tourists.
3. *A Guide to the Great Siberian Railway* issued by the Tsar's government in 1900. It describes scenery, towns, people, and how the railway was built.
4. Prince Yusopov's story of how he murdered Rasputin.
5. Accounts of the royal family and court life by Pierre Gilliard and Sidney Gibbes, Alexei's tutors.
6. The diary kept by the last French ambassador to the Russian court from 1914 to 1918.
7. Governesses' memoirs, and writings by foreign journalists.

I talked to very old Russian friends whose childhood was spent in Nicholas's Russia. They were not in the centre of things but remembered many fascinating little details about life then.

I looked at things dating from Nicholas II's time; old Russian clothes at Luton Hoo in Bedfordshire, beautiful Fabergé Easter eggs, and jewellery owned by the royal family, displayed at the Victoria and Albert Museum in London. In Moscow I went round many ancient churches, monasteries and splendid cathedrals in the Kremlin. In Leningrad (St Petersburg) I saw the dreary, damp cells of the revolutionaries in the Peter and Paul fortress, Prince Yusopov's house, the Winter Palace, and Nicholas's country palace at Tsarskoe Selo. Leningrad has a splendid folk museum containing houses built in the styles of different regions in Russia. All contain their nineteenth-century furniture, and models of villagers wearing working clothes or Sunday best. Here you can see village crafts, and utensils, ranging from bird snares, winter sledges, painted wooden spoons and plaited sandals to pedlars' packs and school textbooks. Moscow also has a whole museum devoted to Lenin, containing his books, letters, clothes, and lots of material about the revolution.

Things to Do

1. Read other books about this time in Russia. You might enjoy
   ROSAMUND DAWE, *A Memoir of an English Governess in Russia*,
   Volume 1 of Unwin Brothers Looking Back Series
   DONALD MACK, *Lenin and the Russian Revolution*, Longman, Then and
   There Series
   E. M. ROBERTS, *Lenin and the Downfall of Tsarist Russia*, Methuen
   JOHN ROBOTTOM, *Modern Russia*, Longman
   SALLY PICKERING, *Twentieth-Century Russia*. Oxford University Press
   DAVID FOOTMAN, *The Russian Revolutions*, Faber
2. Find out more about Witte, Rasputin, Anton Chekhov, Prince
   Yusopov, Lenin and Kerensky
3. Imagine Nicholas II had been brought to trial by the Bolsheviks.
   Arrange a class trial giving the case for and against Nicholas
   as Tsar.
4. Using an atlas and reference books, make a large illustrated wall
   chart showing important places and scenery on the T.S.R. from
   St Petersburg to Vladivistok. Write underneath each place anything interesting you find out.
5. Imagine you are a foreign governess or tutor to children in a noble
   Russian household. Write a letter home describing your ex-
   periences.
6. Make a list of things that English people would have found most
   strange when visiting Nicholas II's Russia. The Then and There
   book on Edwardian England will help to give you the English
   background for comparison.
7. The Russian princesses wrote poems when they were in prison.
   Write one yourself, imagining you are Alexei, or one of the girls
   at Ekaterinburg.
8. For class discussion: Why was there a revolution in Russia in 1917?
   How could it have been avoided?

Glossary

abdicate, give up the throne

accordion, portable musical instrument with a hand bellows and keyboard

amateurish, imperfect, not professional

amnesty, general pardon given to political offenders

analysed, separated into parts and inspected scientifically

assassination, murder, usually of some important person

autocracy, rule by one person

balalaika, Russian musical instrument like a guitar

biased, from one point of view only

bison, large wild animal like a bull

Bolsheviks, Russian revolutionaries following the ideas of Karl Marx. They wanted to overthrow the Tsar's rule by violent means

booze, a drinking session

bombardment, bomb or gun attack

brocade, fine material with raised pattern

cauldron, huge saucepan

caviare, delicacy to eat, made from the roe of the sturgeon (a fish)

censorship, approval or control by public officials

civil war, war between citizens of the same state

communist, one who believes that private property should be abolished and all things held in common

confiscate, take possessions away from owner

congested, overcrowded

convict, a criminal

cossacks, people of south-east Russia forming splendid light horse soldiers

crane, large wading bird with long neck, legs and bill

damask, material of silk, linen or wool with a woven pattern

deacon, a church official, less important than a priest

diplomat, minister in a foreign court; one skilled in drawing up treaties between states *dowager*, title given to a widow to distinguish her from the wife of her husband's heir

dowry, property which a bride brings to her husband on marrying

droshky, Russian cab

Duma, Russian parliament

elder, here means the male leader of a peasant family

emancipation, the act of setting free

emigrant, someone who has moved his home from one country to another

extradited, a criminal being given up to the authorities of the state in which his crime was committed

fake, a sham or swindle

foreboding, a secret sense of some evil happening in the future

galoshes, shoes worn over others in wet weather

governess, a lady who teaches children in their own homes

hostage, one remaining with an enemy as a pledge to fulfil the conditions of a treaty

hypnotic, having the ability to send people to sleep

icon, a figure of Christ or a saint, often painted on wood

iconostasis, wooden screen between the choir and nave of a church on which icons were placed

illiterate, unable to read and write

impartial, not favouring one more than another

impostor, a person pretending to be someone he is not

index finger, finger next to the thumb

interest, money paid for the use of a sum lent

inviolable, that which cannot be injured or harmed

judicial, legal, done by a court of law

kopek, Russian coin of little value

liberal, one who favours freedom

maimed, injured, crippled

manual, handbook

mir, village assembly

morale, confidence, strength of purpose

mosaic, design formed by small pieces of coloured marble or glass cemented on metal or wood

mosque, Muslim place of worship

mutiny, rising against people in authority especially in the army or navy

offensive, attack

Orthodox Church, Eastern Christian church to which Russia belonged

outrage, excessive violence or mischief

ovation, outburst of enthusiastic applause

pedlar, man travelling on foot, and selling small articles

petition, a request, generally from an inferior to a superior

prestige, reputation, influence

prophetic, foreseeing or foretelling events

provisional, temporary, for the time being

redemption taxes, money paid by peasants to the state which had bought land for them

retinue, a body of followers of a person of rank

revolution, violent overthrow of a government

rouble, Russian coin divided into 100 kopeks

sabre, heavy sword used by soldiers on horseback

samovar, Russian tea urn or kettle used for making tea

sea cocks, taps on the pipe which runs from a ship's boiler into the sea

septic, something that speeds up decay

sinister, evil, dishonest

slavonic, belonging to the Slav people

slovenly, disorderly; carelessly or dirtily dressed

Social Democrats, here means a Russian group who followed the writings of Karl Marx

sovereign, old English gold coin worth a pound

soviet, council, usually of workers, soldiers and peasants.

statesmanship, skill in the art of governing

steppe, vast Russian plain

stupor, state of being struck senseless

swaddled, bound tightly with clothes

tarpaulin, strong linen cloth made waterproof by a coating of tar

tiara, ornamental headdress

treaty, agreement signed between one country and another

tutor, private teacher

typhus, easily caught fatal disease often spread in filthy, overcrowded places

unkempt, rough, untidy, dirty

visa, travel document

vodka, Russian drink usually made from rye

wattle, twigs

zemstvo, Russian county council

Index

Acknowledgements

For permission to reproduce photographs we are grateful to the following:

Page:
7 Popperfoto (P.F.)
10 P.F.
17 BBC Hulton Picture Library (B.H.P.L.)
20 B.H.P.L.
22 B.H.P.L.
23 B.H.P.L.
25 B.H.P.L.
26 B.H.P.L.
27 Novosti Press Agency (N.P.A.)
30 B.H.P.L.
36 B.H.P.L.
38 B.H.P.L.
42 *above* P.F.

Page:
42 *below left and right* B.H.P.L.
44 B.H.P.L.
50 N.P.A.
52 B.H.P.L.
58 N.P.A.
61 N.P.A.
62 N.P.A.
65 B.H.P.L.
69 N.P.A.
74 B.H.P.L.
76 N.P.A.
79 P.F.
80 P.F.
85 P.F.

Cover: Novosti Press Agency and Popperfoto.